WRIT OF LOVE

WRIT OF LOVE

by

Cassidy Crane

2024

WRIT OF LOVE

ISBN 13: 978-1-63679-738-0

This Trade Paperback Original Is Published By
Bold Strokes Books, Inc.
P.O. Box 249
Valley Falls, NY 12185

First Edition: October 2024

Credits
Editor: Barbara Ann Wright
Production Design: Stacia Seaman
Cover Design by Jeanine Henning

Acknowledgments

Thank you to all of the wonderful folks at Bold Strokes Books, especially my editor, Barbara Ann Wright.

Thank you to Rachel Manija Brown for suggesting I submit my manuscript to a publisher, and for bravely battling Shelob!

Thank you to my friends for their constant encouragement and moral support. Here's to many more crafternoons, movie nights, and memes to come. Special shout-out to TJ for her unofficial legal advice.

Thank you to my family for always believing in me, and hopefully never reading my books!

I saved the best for last: thank you to my wife for everything. You're the Mike to my Frankie.

For my wife.
Da mi basia mille.

CHAPTER ONE

K elly scrutinized herself in the mirror one more time. Hair, as tamed as it ever was: check. Makeup, subtle and tasteful: check. Suit jacket, buttoned correctly: check. Stewardess-esque scarf, an emergency cover for the love bite on her neck: check.

She sighed, fidgeting with the scarf again. She didn't love it, but it beat showing up for her first day as an associate at the most prestigious law firm in Boston with a bright red hickey. First impressions mattered hugely in the legal field, and she'd rather have people think she was a bit frumpy than the alternative.

She bit her lip as memories from the previous evening flitted across her mind. She still couldn't believe it had really happened, but the mark on her neck was incontrovertible proof that it had. It felt like something someone else had done. Kelly Lattimore always did what was expected of her, putting her most respectable foot forward to best represent both herself and her family. She didn't join gay dating apps, she didn't get seduced by incredibly attractive older women, and she *definitely* didn't have one-night stands.

And yet, she had done all three of those things last night.

She blushed when she thought about it, the noises she'd made and the things she'd said, the uninhibited way she'd let herself have what she wanted without any thought of propriety. With the semblance of anonymity as a security blanket, she'd been able to let go of that controlling voice in her head for a night and give in to her attraction to Jasmine.

Jasmine. Even her name got Kelly feeling hot and bothered again, and she unconsciously rubbed at the hickey on her neck. She dropped her hand as soon as she realized what she was doing, leaving the bathroom in a huff. She was as ready as she'd ever be, and if she lingered much longer, she'd run the risk of being late.

She opted to take a rideshare for her first day; the Boston traffic was even more unpredictable than the T, but at least this way, she didn't have to worry about getting sweaty and disheveled from the crowd of morning commuters packed into under-air-conditioned subway cars. Once she was settled into the back seat of the car with nothing to do but wait to get to work, she found her treacherous brain pulling up last night again like a movie she couldn't look away from.

Maybe you've Found Her? You have one new message in the FindHer app!

Kelly rolled her eyes at the cutesy notification but went right to her inbox on the queer dating app anyway. So far, she'd had a few banal conversations with women she'd felt no chemistry with, deleted messages from half a dozen profiles who'd turned out to be unicorn-hunting hetero couples, and talked with one match, Sam, who'd actually seemed promising.

When Sam had suggested they meet, though, Kelly had gotten cold feet and stopped replying to her. Per an advice blog about hookups, she'd used a fake name, and none of the pictures she'd posted showed her face clearly, but actually getting together for coffee felt too real, too exposing.

Besides, Kelly wasn't at a point in her life where she was looking for a relationship anyway. A casual hookup should have been enough for what she needed to know. As confident as she was that she was probably somewhere on the queer spectrum, it would be incontrovertible evidence to herself, depending on how it went.

The new message was from someone named Jasmine. Her profile picture was so zoomed in that it was hard to make out her face, which was half covered by giant sunglasses. From what Kelly could see, though, she looked pretty enough.

Jasmine: *I had a great opening line ready, but you're so hot I've forgotten it.*

Kelly laughed, but her cheeks heated up at the silly message anyway. She decided Jasmine had earned a reply for sending something more creative than the usual boring "hi, how are you" opening, and tried to write a response that matched the lighthearted, flirty tone.

Eleanor: *I don't usually give compliments right away, but you have excellent taste in women.*

Jasmine must have been online, because she replied almost immediately. *I'm free tonight if you want to grab a drink.*

Eleanor: *I'd hate to think of you sitting home alone, pining for me.*

Kelly could hardly believe her own daring. She should have dropped this immediately, unmatched from Jasmine and gone to bed early. She had a big day tomorrow, after all. Even if she went through with it and actually met Jasmine, there was no way she would be able to keep this up in person. She just knew she'd get all tongue-tied and shy and wind up disappointing Jasmine. She started mentally drafting a polite end to the conversation, still feeling guilty about how she'd ghosted Sam, but Jasmine responded first.

Jasmine: *See how lonely I am? I need you to keep me company.*

Below the message, she'd included a picture that made Kelly's jaw drop. Jasmine had taken it of herself from the neck down, lying on a bed wearing nothing but lacy black lingerie. One of her hands had dipped inside her panties, pulling them tantalizingly low on her hips.

Eleanor: *When and where?*

❖

The lighting was dim enough that it took Kelly's eyes a minute or two to adjust when she entered the popular gay bar an hour later. She headed straight for the bar, ordered an overpriced glass of pinot grigio, and chugged most of it to try to calm the nerves caroming around in her head. It sort of worked. At any rate, she surveyed the room looking for Jasmine while sipping the rest of the wine instead of barreling for the exit.

Although it was still fairly early, the place was packed and noisy. As she raised her glass to her lips, someone jostled her elbow, and she nearly spilled her drink. A group of women on their way to the bathroom had swarmed past her and didn't seem to even notice they'd bumped into her. It reminded Kelly why she usually stayed away from bars, but hopefully, tonight would be worth it.

Her eyes landed on a woman a few seats away and just about popped out of her head. It was hard to tell in the low light, but she was maybe eight or ten years older than Kelly. Her black sequined dress was long-sleeved, but its short skirt and plunging neckline left little to the imagination. Her dark hair was tied back in an elegant updo, except for one tendril that she kept twirling around her finger as she flirted with the bartender.

Kelly felt a swirl of lust as she watched her. The woman looked up and caught her eye, and Kelly's whole body froze as adrenaline flooded her system.

"Eleanor?" the woman asked, arching her eyebrows.

For a second, Kelly forgot the fake name she'd given on the app and merely stared at her dumbly. "Uh, yeah, that's me," she said. "I take it you're Jasmine?"

"Right in one," Jasmine said, smiling at her in a way that made Kelly's stomach swoop.

Kelly rose shakily from her stool and went to sit down next to Jasmine, her pulse thudding in her ears.

"What do you think of the place?" Jasmine asked.

Kelly bit her lip, not wanting to insult it when Jasmine had been the one to suggest it. "It definitely wasn't what I expected when I came here. I thought it would be…well, I don't know, but it's just like any other bar, too many drunk people," she said at last.

Jasmine smiled and took a swig from her glass. "You can't have been to *that* many bars. What are you, twenty-two?"

"Twenty-five, actually," Kelly told her. "But you're right, I don't really hang around bars that much. Like I said, too many drunk people."

"Smart girl," Jasmine said approvingly, and Kelly felt a surprising surge of pleasure. She wanted to hear this woman compliment her in an entirely different context, and she realized she was getting turned on from literally two words. Apparently, she had a bit of a praise kink. "Can I get you a drink?"

"Thank you," Kelly said. She could feel herself starting to flush under the weight of Jasmine's gaze.

Jasmine gestured to the bartender, who soon brought over two more of the deep red cocktails she had been drinking. "It's cranberry and soda water," Jasmine explained when she saw Kelly eyeing it. "I don't drink."

"So naturally, you suggested meeting up in a bar," Kelly said sarcastically without thinking, then clapped a hand over her mouth in horror at her own rudeness.

Rather than being offended, Jasmine laughed, looking delighted. "I misread you. You seemed a little buttoned-up and shy, but you've got a bit of an attitude going on under there, don't you?" She ran a finger slowly across Kelly's bare forearm.

Kelly took a sip of her drink to avoid answering right away. Her body's reaction to Jasmine's mild compliment was nothing compared to what it was doing now. The spot on her arm where Jasmine had touched felt like it had been burned. "Still waters run deep, I guess," she said at last.

Jasmine smirked, then sighed. "If you really want to know, my divorce just got finalized on Friday, and I suggested this place to...celebrate, I suppose, although that's a weird word for it. Let's be real, we're both here to get laid. Where else are we going to meet than in a bar?"

"That's pretty sound reasoning," Kelly said, realizing Jasmine was studying her out of the corner of her eye.

Jasmine looked at her head-on now and continued, "I'm going to be completely level with you here. I'm not looking for a relationship right now. At all. And you're way too young for me anyway. But since you said in your profile that you're only interested in a casual thing right now...I'm offering."

Kelly gaped at her. She felt the blush rise all the way to her ears, but she was powerless to stop it. She tried to form words, but her brain wouldn't cooperate.

"Did I break you? Never mind," Jasmine said, watching her with some concern.

"No, I just…I haven't done this before, and you're very… forthright," Kelly said, still flushed.

Jasmine shrugged. "One thing you learn when you get divorced is that life's really fucking short. I'm horny, you're hot, and I'd show you a good time. But if you're not up for that, no worries. We can just talk here, or I can leave you alone, and you never have to talk to me again."

Kelly drank some more of her mocktail and thought hard. She'd never had a one-night stand before, but she couldn't deny how attracted she was to Jasmine. Jasmine wasn't promising anything more than a hookup, but wasn't that what she wanted, too?

Finally she nodded and said, "Okay."

"Are you sure?" Jasmine asked intently. "Because I definitely don't want to pressure you. I feel like enough of a creep hitting on a twenty-five-year-old as it is."

"How old are *you*?" Kelly asked, realizing it was a slightly rude question but wanting to know anyway.

"Forty-five," Jasmine said with a wince.

Kelly stared at her in surprise. "No way! I thought you were, like, thirty-five at most."

Jasmine's eyebrows rose. "Well, that's very flattering. But if that, you know, changes your mind…" It was the first time since they'd met that she had seemed anything but entirely self-possessed.

"It doesn't," Kelly said firmly. "I've never done anything like this, which you could probably already tell, but…you're hot too, and I want to."

Jasmine laughed. "See how much easier it is when we're both up-front with each other?"

"It really is," Kelly agreed. "So, um, do you want to go to your place? I have a roommate."

"Let's definitely go to mine, then," Jasmine said with a shudder. "I do *not* miss those days."

❖

Jasmine drove them in her sleek, expensive-looking car. Once they were on the way, the enormity of what she was doing sank in a little, and Kelly found herself getting quiet once more. Thankfully, Jasmine's swanky apartment building wasn't far away, and soon, they were pulling into an underground parking garage. As they rode the elevator up to Jasmine's top-floor apartment, she asked, "How much did you have to drink tonight? I didn't think about that before."

"Only one glass of wine when I first got to the bar. I'm not drunk, if that's what you're worried about," Kelly said. It was true; the slight buzz she'd gotten after drinking the first glass so quickly had faded, and she was, if anything, a little *too* sober now for her preference. She could have used something to take the edge off. She knew she wanted this, but it was hard to silence the little voice in her head that sounded like her mother, admonishing her not to do anything that might embarrass the Lattimore family. She tried not to think about her mother's reaction if she knew what her daughter was planning to do tonight.

"Okay, just making sure. I want you to remember every single thing I do to you tonight," Jasmine said in her ear as the elevator dinged. Kelly fought back a whimper of mingled anxiety and arousal as Jasmine led the way to her front door and let them inside.

"Whoa," Kelly said, forgetting her nerves at the sight of

the floor to ceiling windows looking out over the harbor. It was pretty enough now, with lights twinkling from the boats moored below; the view in daylight would be spectacular.

Jasmine grinned. "Yeah, that's why I picked this place."

"It's nice," Kelly said, finally looking around at the interior of Jasmine's home. She was curious to see what she could glean about the woman she'd be spending the night with. The apartment was beautiful, to be sure, with high-end furnishings and gleaming granite countertops. There were no personal touches at all, though. It might as well have been a hotel suite for all it told her about Jasmine as a person.

Jasmine seemed to sense her reaction. "I just moved in. My ex and I were sharing custody of our townhouse downtown. We each spent a week there and then a week in a hotel, switching back and forth, but she got it in the divorce settlement. I don't miss *her*, but I do miss the house. You want character, that place has it in spades." She heaved a sigh and flung her purse on an armchair. "Anyway, you don't want to hear about all that. Can I get you anything? Water?"

"No, I'm good," Kelly said, dropping her purse next to Jasmine's.

"Oh, that remains to be seen," Jasmine murmured with a smirk, stepping closer.

Kelly bit her lip as what felt like all the blood in her body rushed southward. "Why don't you come find out?" she whispered.

Jasmine crossed the space between them in milliseconds. She was a few inches shorter than Kelly but in complete control as she tugged her into a rough kiss. Kelly melted under her touch, unable to do anything but kiss her back for all she was worth. Jasmine's hand slid to the back of her neck as her tongue entered Kelly's mouth. Kelly sighed with pleasure, dropping her hands to rest on Jasmine's waist. Finally they broke apart, both breathing heavily. Wordlessly, Jasmine grabbed her hand and pulled her down the hallway to the bedroom.

Jasmine kissed her again, and Kelly returned it eagerly, relishing the feel of her lips, the little hitch in her breath when Jasmine's tongue slipped into her mouth. Jasmine's hands moved to the hem of her shirt, and Kelly lifted her arms so she could pull it off and toss it carelessly onto the floor. Her hands immediately started roaming all over Kelly's body, and Kelly moaned helplessly as Jasmine unhooked her bra and took her nipple into her mouth. She ran her tongue all over it before tugging at it gently with her teeth.

"That feels amazing," Kelly breathed, watching with wide eyes as Jasmine repeated the action on the other side. Pleasure rushed through her, and she felt almost painfully turned on. Jasmine looked up at her and smiled wickedly, running her hands up her skirt and caressing her thighs.

Kelly started to reach under Jasmine's skirt in turn, but Jasmine stopped her. "I want you to come for me at least twice before I let you touch me."

Her words sent a thrill and an absolute tidal wave of wetness to Kelly's core, and all she could do was whimper. Jasmine looked at her questioningly. "Is this okay? Just tell me if anything is too much, or you want to stop," she said.

"Yes, yes it's okay," Kelly whispered. She was in way over her head, but that had been true all evening, and she was far too turned on to stop now.

"For the second one, I'd really like to fuck you, but I think I'll let you choose for the first time," Jasmine said conversationally. "Do you want my hand? Do you want me to eat you out? Tell me what you like."

Kelly's brain short-circuited at first, overwhelmed by the

lurid images now flashing through her mind. Finally, she said quietly, "I want...I want it all. You can decide."

Jasmine's dark eyes flashed hungrily. "Oh, you *are* a delight. As soon as I saw you, I knew I was going to ghost poor Eleanor if you weren't her."

It might have been an invention of her lust-addled brain, but Kelly was pretty sure Jasmine was admitting to checking her out before they'd even spoken. The thought of Jasmine wanting her on sight made her gasp, and she couldn't scramble onto the bed fast enough.

Jasmine straddled her, the skirt of her dress hiked up to her hips. Her thighs were creamy and smooth, and Kelly wanted her mouth on them more than she'd ever wanted anything, but she knew she'd have to wait. Jasmine looked at her for a moment, devouring her with her eyes. She gently held Kelly's hands above her head as she lowered herself on top of her, her mouth suddenly everywhere: her lips, the hollow of her throat, lavishing attention on her nipples. Kelly moaned, thrusting her body against Jasmine's above her. The sequins of Jasmine's dress were prickly against her bare torso, but that only added to the sensual onslaught.

Jasmine pressed her lips to Kelly's neck and sucked hard. There was an audible popping noise as she pulled away, and too late, Kelly realized the risk. "Wait! Don't leave a mark, I start my new job tomorrow."

"Oops," Jasmine said. "Nothing else visible, got it. Sorry about that."

"It's okay, just keep touching me, *please*," Kelly panted.

"Fuck, you're delicious," Jasmine muttered. "Since you asked so sweetly..." She cupped Kelly's breasts, massaging her nipples until she was crying out and grinding her hips against Jasmine's again.

Jasmine rolled down beside her and pulled Kelly to face her. Her hands roamed freely over Kelly's body, eagerly helping her shed the rest of her clothes, cupping her ass, scratching her nails down her bare back. Kelly's senses were on fire, every nerve ending crying out with pleasure and want. Jasmine seemed content to tease her, touching seemingly every inch of her body except where she wanted her the most. She sucked on her nipples again until Kelly felt almost delirious with aching need, then slid two fingers inside her but refused to touch her clit. Kelly whimpered in dismay.

"Maybe if you ask nicely," Jasmine said. "I know you can."

"Please, please, please," Kelly said through gritted teeth.

"Please what?" Jasmine asked idly, as if Kelly's plight bored her. Kelly didn't know why that was working for her, but she'd never been more turned on in her life.

"Please let me come," she begged. Something flashed in Jasmine's eyes, and she knew she was finally about to get the release her body was crying out for.

Jasmine nodded, but she moved away from her. Kelly whimpered again, and Jasmine grinned at her. "I love to hear you so desperate and begging," she said. She rummaged in her nightstand drawer and returned to her previous position holding a bright pink vibrator. Kelly could see that Jasmine's fingers were shiny and wet with her arousal, and it made her body clench painfully, needing them back inside her. Jasmine seemed to read her mind, and she sighed in relief as Jasmine's fingers started fucking her in earnest. With her other hand she clicked the vibrator on and moved it over her clit.

Kelly wasn't sure, but it was possible she blacked out for a second. Every nerve in her body was shrieking out in overwhelming pleasure. Vaguely, she heard someone chanting,

"Oh fuck, oh my God," over and over again, and realized the words were coming from her own mouth as she rocked her hips against Jasmine's fingers. It felt like the sensation went on forever, and she was gasping for breath when it finally faded.

When she looked over at Jasmine, she saw she was licking Kelly's wetness off her fingers. Jasmine caught her eye. "You really are delicious," she purred. "I kind of regret not using my mouth instead."

Her words and the visual sent another lightning bolt of lust rocketing through Kelly's body, which she wouldn't have thought possible after the mind-blowing orgasm she'd just had. She moved over to Jasmine and kissed her hungrily.

When Jasmine finally pulled away, she cupped Kelly's cheek. The sudden moment of tenderness threw her for a loop, and she could only stare as Jasmine looked at her searchingly. "Are you good? That wasn't too much, was it?"

Kelly shook her head, surprised Jasmine needed to ask. "No, it was…amazing," she said shyly.

"Okay, good," Jasmine said. "Because if you want to stop or anything…"

"Why would I want to stop?" Kelly asked, baffled.

Jasmine shrugged. "Just, if that was too intense or something. I don't know if you're the type who'll actually say something if I start going too far."

"Well, I am," Kelly told her. "But since you're worried about it, I'll be as clear as I can. I believe you said something about fucking me for round two?"

Jasmine eyed her hopefully. "Do you want that?"

Kelly nodded. "I want you to wreck me," she whispered.

"Fuck," Jasmine said, her eyes fluttering shut for a moment. "I knew you'd be a dirty girl. You look so squeaky clean and pure, but underneath, you're just dying to be corrupted."

The words sent another surge of desire coursing through Kelly's veins. In answer, she rolled onto her back and spread her legs.

Jasmine inhaled sharply at the sight. "God, you're just about the hottest thing I've ever seen," she said, staring at Kelly as though transfixed.

Kelly arched an eyebrow. "Are you going to sit there all night, or are you going to fuck me?" She didn't know what had come over her; she'd never been this uninhibited in bed, but her desire for Jasmine seemed to be overriding all her sense of shame or embarrassment.

The look Jasmine gave her felt like it shot straight through her soul. "I stand corrected. You're *already* quite a dirty girl, aren't you?"

"Only for you," Kelly said quietly.

Jasmine smirked. "That's right. We still might have to do something about that mouth of yours, though."

"I wish you would."

"Fucking hell," Jasmine said. "Okay, you asked for it. Unzip me."

Kelly dutifully undid the zipper at the back of Jasmine's dress. She tried to use the excuse of helping her take it off to cop a feel of her cleavage, but Jasmine was on to her and slapped her hand away. It didn't really hurt, but the sharp smacking sound was enough to make her moan. She moaned again when Jasmine shrugged her shoulders and let the dress fall to the ground, showing off the lacy black plunge bra and matching panties from the picture she'd sent earlier.

"I don't want to hear another word out of you without permission," Jasmine said sternly, and Kelly nodded. Her mouth went dry as she watched Jasmine pull what she needed out of the nightstand, shuck her panties, and start buckling on the harness. A pressing wave of want surged through her body as Jasmine climbed back onto the bed. She caressed Kelly's thighs with the gentlest of touches, then ran her fingers sensuously between her legs. Kelly gasped and ground her hips against Jasmine's hand.

"Ah, ah, ah, that's enough of that," Jasmine said, taking her hand away. A second later, she was easing the strap-on inside, and Kelly let out a deep breath to relax her muscles and let it in. She gasped with pleasure as Jasmine slid farther in. The feeling of being slowly filled was exquisite. Once Jasmine was fully inside her, Kelly pulled her in for a kiss.

"Baby, you take it so well for me," Jasmine said as she pulled out and drove back in. She stuck two fingers in Kelly's mouth for her to suck. Kelly moaned around Jasmine's fingers and dug her nails into her back, urging her on. "Fuck, oh fuck, you're such a good girl for me," Jasmine went on, sliding in and out. Kelly cried out wordlessly as Jasmine rubbed at her clit with her hand, and sparks of pleasure shot through her body.

Jasmine lifted Kelly's leg up to her shoulder to drive in deeper. Kelly's breath was coming in desperate little gasps as Jasmine kept fucking into her. She could hear Jasmine's skin slapping against hers with every thrust.

"Tell me how much you love it," Jasmine panted, pulling her fingers out of Kelly's mouth as she pounded into her again and again.

"I do, I love it, you're so good to me, you're the best, oh fuck, give it to me," Kelly babbled, feeling herself on the cusp.

Jasmine drove in deep, panting from the sustained effort. "That's it, baby, come for me," she murmured, and Kelly did, crying out incoherently as wave after wave of her orgasm washed over her. She pumped her hips against Jasmine, dragging out every last bit of pleasure she could. Her mind was hazy, and she felt like she was floating when she sank back into the pillow, deliciously sore and finally spent.

Jasmine flopped down next to her, trying to catch her breath. "I think I made the right choice tonight," she said, brushing Kelly's sweaty hair out of her eyes.

"I agree," Kelly said, giggling. She reached down and tried to undo the strap-on harness for Jasmine, but either her brain was still a little foggy or it was too complicated to do by feel alone.

Jasmine laughed softly. "Here, allow me," she said, unbuckling it and tossing it aside with a flourish.

Kelly wondered how many women she'd used it on to be so adept with it, then banished the thought. It was none of her business anyway. Instead, she asked, "Can I go down on you?" It was something she'd fantasized about for years, and she wasn't about to pass up the opportunity to finally experience it.

"I think I just might be able to find it in me to let you," Jasmine said dryly.

"You're so generous," Kelly said.

Jasmine laughed. "Don't say I never gave you anything."

"I mean, you've already given me two fairly excellent orgasms, so I couldn't in good conscience say that anyway," Kelly said.

She rolled onto her stomach as Jasmine lay back and opened her legs. Kelly took a deep breath and settled herself between them. She was transfixed by the beauty of the sight in front of her. Jasmine's thighs looked as luscious as ever, and her center was shiny with arousal. Kelly felt her mouth water looking at it. She mouthed kisses along Jasmine's thighs, which were just as silky soft as she thought they'd be.

She took a deep breath to steady her nerves, then took a tentative first lick. She repeated the action with a little more confidence, and Jasmine rewarded her with a gasp. She tried different places and angles, going back over and over again to the places that got the loudest reactions. Unsurprisingly, sucking on her clit seemed to be particularly enjoyable, but she also got especially loud whenever Kelly dropped her tongue to probe at her entrance. She'd worried the reality wouldn't live up to her fantasy, but it turned out she loved it more than she could have imagined. The taste, the smell, the heat of Jasmine's wet folds, and the little whimpering sounds Jasmine was making were impossibly erotic. She kept going, and Jasmine buried her hands in Kelly's hair and rolled her hips gently against her face, moaning with pleasure.

"Oh my fucking God, baby, you're so good at that," Jasmine groaned. "You were fucking born to eat pussy." Kelly moaned at the words, and Jasmine reacted even louder to the vibration. A minute later she was coming, and Kelly gripped her thighs tight and let her ride it out against her face.

After Jasmine was finished, she stared at the ceiling and said, "I think you broke my brain."

"In a good way, I hope," Kelly said, lying down next to her.

Jasmine finally turned to look at her. "In a very good way. That was just what I needed."

Kelly smiled, but now that the sex part was done, she was starting to feel awkward. She was already embarrassed by how openly she'd expressed her desire to someone she barely knew. She didn't know if she was supposed to stay overnight or even linger at all, and if so, for how long. She hadn't thought this part through when she'd decided to come home with Jasmine, and she certainly wasn't about to reveal her inexperience by asking. She'd just have to follow Jasmine's lead.

Jasmine was aimlessly trailing her fingers along Kelly's stomach. "So," she said, "I have an early day tomorrow, and you're starting a new job, right? It might be best if I got you an Uber, and that way, we can both get a good night's sleep."

Well, that answered that question. Apparently, Jasmine expected her to leave almost immediately. That was probably for the best. Trying to linger risked muddying the waters, perhaps making her think that Kelly was trying to push for more. Jasmine walked her down to the lobby and gave her a slightly stilted hug good-bye when her car arrived. She didn't ask for Kelly's number, and Kelly didn't offer it. Jasmine had been very clear that this was a one-time thing, and she obviously meant it.

CHAPTER TWO

M s. Briggs? It's Mr. Sullivan, and he says it's urgent."
Jillian groaned. "What is it this time, he can't find a stapler? I swear, that man would lose his own dick if it wasn't attached to his body."

Ezra choked on the other end of the phone. "He's actually here. In person. Right in front of me. Should I send him in?"

Shit. Jillian prayed to whatever deities there might be that Ezra was using his headset and not speakerphone. "Yes, by all means. Why not," she said with a sigh. What a great start to a Monday.

Seconds later, Thomas Sullivan entered her office. Although he wasn't technically her boss, as a senior partner in the litigation division, he had considerable sway over her standing in the firm and wasn't someone she could afford to offend. After ten years as a partner, she was so close to finally being in the top echelon.

"Good morning, Jillian," he said jovially.

"Ah, good morning, Tom," she said, hoisting her most professional smile onto her face. He tended to play his cards close to his chest, so she couldn't tell whether he'd overheard her remark to Ezra. "Can I have Ezra get you anything? Coffee?"

"No time," he said, waving off the offer. "It really is urgent. The first-year associates start today, and Leon Marsh broke his ankle falling downstairs this morning. You may know we're trying out a new model of associate training by pairing them up with a partner for two weeks, and Leon's going to be out for that whole time. I need someone to show his new associate the ropes. He suggested you."

Only years of practice at keeping her face tightly controlled kept Jillian from grimacing in horror. There were few things she hated more than breaking in brand-new associates. It was a fairly thankless task, one she dodged whenever possible. The worst part was when some bratty little Ivy League grad who'd coasted his whole life on Daddy's name and money inevitably tried to challenge her knowledge or authority. She'd worked her ass off to come as far as she had, and she had to work twice as hard to stay there. It would only take a few murmurings about how *Briggs isn't logging quite as many billable hours as she used to* in order to set her back years.

"Poor Leon," she said as sincerely as she could manage. *He'll be far worse off than a broken ankle by the time I get him back for this.* Their mutual animosity stretched back years to when he had all but accused her of sleeping with half the senior partners in the firm when she'd made partner before he had. She just knew he'd prodded Tom to dump the new associate on her out of spite.

"I'm not sure I'm the best choice for that, though," she said to Tom. "I'm up to my eyeballs in depositions for the Glickman case, and besides, I haven't done it in quite a while. I'm sure I'm rusty. How about Chris Hendricks or Elliot Springman?" If she managed to fob this off on either of them, she'd find a way to make up for it later.

Tom gave one of his sharklike smiles that didn't reach his eyes. "No, I think you're exactly the best choice, Jillian.

After all, as you say, you haven't done it in a while, and we all need to pull our weight around here. Plus, it'll be a good learning experience for the new associate." His tone brooked no argument, and she knew the battle was lost.

"Besides," he added as he headed to the door, "it'd be impossible for me to *find* anyone else to do it at this point. Carol in HR is sending them all up at nine." With that, he walked away without a second glance.

Jillian waited until the door swung shut behind him, then thunked her head gently on her desk while muttering "Fuckety fuck fuck."

The door squeaked open again, and Ezra hurried in. "Ms. Briggs, I'm *so* sorry about that. He snuck up on me before I had my Bluetooth hooked up, and I know I should have warned you but—"

"It's okay, Ezra, it's not your fault," she said, holding up a hand. It was always best to cut him off as soon as possible on one of his rambling apologies; otherwise, he could go on all day. She sent him off to find her some Advil instead.

She gripped the bridge of her nose between her thumb and forefinger. She could already feel a headache starting to form. The last thing she needed today was some inexperienced brand-new lawyer slowing her down. She couldn't believe she'd actually been in a good mood this morning. She'd had good reasons for that, though. It was her first day back as an officially single woman, no more divorce proceedings hanging over her head, no more worrying about whether Tessa would drop by the office just to pick a fight. By the time they had called it quits for good, she'd been hiding at work so much that those office arguments were practically the only time they saw each other.

The other reason for her good mood was the delightful way she'd spent Sunday evening. She'd resorted to the app, hoping that a bout or two of meaningless sex would be just what she needed to kick off her post-divorce life, and she'd gotten so much more than she'd bargained for.

She'd felt Eleanor's eyes on her almost the minute she'd entered the bar. The attention was certainly a nice ego boost, but she didn't usually go for the prudish ingenue type. At first glance, that description had fitted Eleanor to a T, with her preppy clothes, neat blond bob, and wide hazel eyes. But there was something indefinable about her that told Jillian she was different, that underneath that prim exterior was a passionate lover begging to be set free. She could never have predicted how right she'd be.

Eleanor had certainly seemed to have a good time too, and Jillian felt a stab of regret at not getting her number. She wouldn't have minded repeating the experience. But, she reminded herself, that was exactly her problem with everything, wasn't it? Always wanting more, never letting anything be enough. It was called a *one*-night stand for a reason, even if that one night had included some of the hottest sex of her life. The one bright side she could see was that she never had to worry about wanting too much from Eleanor because most likely, she'd never see her again. Still, she couldn't help thinking about last night again, the noises she'd wrung out of Eleanor, how avidly Eleanor had gone down on her…

Ezra returned with her Advil, snapping her out of her reverie. "The new associates are already downstairs with Carol. They'll be up here any minute," he said. "Mr. Marsh's assistant sent over his new associate's file for you. It's at the top of your inbox."

Jillian groaned and accepted the pills. "Okay, let's get this over with. I swear, if this snot-nosed little shit tries to test me today, I'm canning his ass on the spot."

Timidly, Ezra said, "Um, actually Ms. Briggs, only Mr. Sullivan has the authority—"

"I know, Ezra," Jillian said, managing to keep the bite of impatience out of her voice. "It's called hyperbole, and it's one of my coping mechanisms."

She heard the ding of the elevator out on the main floor and then the clicking of heels and dress shoes on the marble tile as the new associates were distributed to the partners they'd be assisting. She took a deep breath and donned the veneer of unflappable poise and control that had carried her this far in her career. Intimidating the new associates was one of the unspoken rules of the training process, and she had no intention of breaking that tradition.

She pulled up Ezra's email and scanned the new associate's resume. The name Kelly Lattimore jumped out at her, and she wondered if she was dealing with someone from *the* Lattimore family. Between the various branches of their family tree, they probably owned half the city. That pedigree, combined with a BA from Yale and a JD from Harvard, a stint as law review editor, and a prestigious summer internship with a state supreme court justice while in law school all but guaranteed this one would be an obnoxious douchebag.

There was a timid knock in her doorway, and she looked up.

Oh God, it was Eleanor. What the fuck was she doing here? She'd seemed totally fine when she'd left last night, but was she turning out to be a crazy stalker? Jillian reached for her phone to tell Ezra to have security on standby when she noticed the staff badge pinned to Eleanor's lapel with *Kelly Lattimore* in big letters.

She was staring at Jillian from the doorway, her hazel eyes huge. Jillian remembered Eleanor saying she was starting a new job today and noticed the little scarf she had tied around her neck covering the hickey Jillian had left. What a great fucking joke the universe was playing on her. So much for never seeing Eleanor—no, Kelly—again. They'd be spending every day of the next two weeks together.

Blood was thundering in her ears. It took every ounce of self-control she possessed, but Jillian was pretty sure she managed a neutral smile. "Well, hello. This is quite unexpected."

"Um. Uh. Um. Hi?" Kelly said, still looking like a deer in headlights.

"Come in, have a seat. Shut the door behind you. We need to talk," Jillian said, gesturing to the seat opposite her desk.

"Are you going to fire me?" Kelly asked quietly as she sat.

Jillian raised her eyebrows. "Yes, because I, a partner in the *litigation division*, am stupid enough to expose this firm to the slam dunk lawsuit that would create."

Kelly flushed. "Okay, I deserved that. But what's going to happen?"

"Here's what we're going to do," Jillian said, steepling her fingers. "Last night never happened. Tell your therapist if you need to tell *someone*, but not another living soul can find out about this. We'll get through the next two weeks, and once Leon's back, we'll never work together again. I'd try to get you reassigned until then, but I'm already on thin ice with Tom Sullivan after this morning, so there's no way he'd say yes without knowing what happened."

"We didn't do anything wrong," Kelly said, chewing on her lip nervously. "I mean, I didn't know who you were, and you didn't know who I was, and I wasn't even technically working here yet, and you aren't even my permanent supervisor—"

Kelly could give Ezra a run for his money at anxious

babbling. She didn't show any signs of slowing down, so Jillian just started talking over her. "It's not in either of our best interests for anyone to know about this. The extenuating circumstances won't matter. Things have gotten a little better for women since I started out, but believe me when I say that something like this will follow you around for the rest of your time at this firm if it ever gets out, probably your entire career. Not to mention mine. Your family might be able to shield you from some of the fallout, but I don't have that luxury. I've worked too damn hard to get where I am for you to mess it up. Is that clear?"

"Crystal," Kelly said quietly.

"Excellent, let's get started," Jillian said briskly, clapping her hands. She picked up her phone again. "Ezra, can you bring in a copy of the Glickman files for Kelly? There's no time to waste."

Chapter Three

Kelly looked at Jillian in mute horror. Not twelve hours ago, she'd been naked in her temporary new boss's bed, begging her to fuck her. This had to be a nightmare; that was the only explanation. Jillian's eyes had widened slightly when she first saw Kelly, and she'd paused for a millisecond, but other than that, she'd showed no reaction other than mild surprise. Kelly wished she had half of Jillian's wherewithal. When Jillian's assistant brought the files in, he did a double take after he looked at Kelly, and she knew her face must be doing something weird.

"I have a deposition this afternoon. You're coming with me but for observational purposes only. You're not to speak for any reason," Jillian said, eyeing her sternly.

Kelly nodded, uncomfortably reminded of when Jillian had told her not to speak without permission in a very different context last night. She wondered if Jillian remembered.

"And I mean *any* reason," Jillian continued. "If you notice the building's on fire, tap me on the shoulder and point."

"I get it. No talking," Kelly said, keeping her tone as neutral as possible. Did Jillian think she was a complete idiot? She'd heard her the first time.

Jillian eyed her suspiciously but moved on. "The opposing counsel isn't a total waste of space, so pay attention to his objections, especially when he tries to steer his client away from danger zones. That's where we want to dig in. Take lots of notes."

The morning flew by in a haze. Kelly managed to stay focused on the case through a combination of sheer force of will and fear of embarrassment at being caught in a moment of inattention. Jillian's client was an advertising company being sued for copyright violations, and she expected the plaintiff would soon drop the case. Until that happened, though, they had to assume it would go to trial and act accordingly. She gave Kelly a very rough overview of the facts of the case but expected her to spend her lunch hour speed-reading all the background material before the deposition.

Kelly found many of her fellow new associates looking similarly shell-shocked in the break room at noon. All of them were carrying huge stacks of paperwork and wearing matching expressions of terror, which made her feel a little better. Sure, probably none of them had the added awkwardness of having slept with their new bosses the night before, but other than that, they were all in the same boat. She sat with a few people she knew from law school, but they were all too busy shoving hurried bites of lunch into their mouths while poring over legal documents to talk.

Kelly took two minutes she didn't really have to read Jillian's profile on the firm's website before the deposition. She kicked herself for not having done it earlier, but she'd simply run out of time before starting. She'd meant to read up on all the partners, but the firm was massive, and there were nearly a hundred partners at this location alone.

If anything, she was even more intimidated about working

with Jillian after reading more about her. No wonder she was so protective of her career; she had been the youngest female partner in the firm's history and had an enormous number of impressive legal victories under her belt. If it weren't for last night, Kelly would have been over the moon at the opportunity to learn from her and watch her in action. Maybe she could start by emulating Jillian's impressive compartmentalization skills and try to act like nothing had happened.

She and Jillian rode the elevator together down to the conference room where the deposition was being held. It was another reminder of the night before, but Kelly batted the thought away.

"What are you going to be doing during the deposition?" Jillian asked as the doors closed.

"Taking notes and not talking," Kelly said.

Jillian nodded. "Sometimes, there's an associate who thinks they're the exception and tries to get cute. You are not the exception. You'll embarrass yourself, you'll embarrass me, and you'll embarrass the firm."

I already know you think I'm cute, though. But she knew better than to say it out loud. In truth, she was starting to feel a little irritated, but she tried to hide it. "I really do get it. I promise, I'm not going to say anything."

Kelly walked half a step behind Jillian as they made their way to the conference room. Jillian's strides were long and purposeful, and she seemed utterly unselfconscious about how loudly her heels were clacking on the floor. Even though her legs were longer, Kelly had to increase her pace to keep up. When they reached the glass-walled conference room, she narrowed her eyes at Kelly in a final warning before pulling the door open and leading the way in.

Kelly couldn't help but be wryly amused when Jillian introduced her as "one of our brightest rising stars," considering that she didn't seem to think Kelly was capable of following the simplest instructions.

Once the deposition began, though, she was far too busy for such thoughts. She took notes like Jillian had told her to, her fingers flying over the keyboard. It was fascinating to watch Jillian work up close. She started off with softball questions, eventually leading the smug wannabe Don Draper she was deposing into admitting that he hadn't even designed his ad campaign until after her client's TV commercial had aired. It was so gradual that neither Kelly nor the advertiser's lawyer realized what she was doing until it was too late.

Jillian went preternaturally still for a moment, but that was the only reaction she showed. If Kelly hadn't been embarrassingly attuned to Jillian's body beside her, she doubted she would have even noticed. The other lawyer turned a remarkable shade of red when he realized what had just happened, and he barely spoke to either of them as he ushered his client out when the deposition was finished. Jillian waited until the court reporter had packed up her equipment and bid them farewell before breaking out into a Cheshire Cat smile.

"That was unbelievable," Kelly said quietly, hoping she was allowed to talk now.

Jillian beamed at her, and her heart skipped a beat. "And *that's* how you depose a witness. Did you see their faces?"

"He was so busy trying to prove how much more he knew about advertising than you that he walked right into your trap," Kelly said.

Jillian raised her eyebrows. "That *was* my strategy, yeah. You catch on quick. Maybe you got hired for more than your family connections after all."

Kelly winced at the reference to her family. If Jillian knew the truth… "Actually, about that—"

"Stop, I don't care," Jillian said curtly. "Meet me back

in my office in ten minutes. We'll go over your notes, and I need you to do some research for another case. Don't plan on leaving before ten tonight."

She marched away, and Kelly sighed as she watched her go. She supposed she'd better get used to late nights. She'd known what she was signing up for, going into Big Law, but that didn't make it any more pleasant.

Jillian pronounced her deposition notes "not bad" and had only a few criticisms, which she chose to take as a win. At the very least, she hadn't totally embarrassed herself. Late afternoon melted into evening as she holed up in the library doing the research Jillian wanted and trying to formulate it into a reasonably coherent report. She hadn't been this tired and stressed since her first semester of law school.

At seven, Ezra messaged her that he was going home but gave her instructions on how to order dinner on the firm's account. She gratefully fell on the mountain of Chinese food she had delivered, then went back to work. She read and wrote for hours, until the words on the page started dancing in front of her eyes. She realized she'd been trying to read the same page of the treatise she was looking at several times and hadn't taken in a single word. She stared at it again, her eyelids growing heavy.

The next thing she knew, someone was gently shaking her shoulder. "Kelly, wake up."

"Bwa?" she said blearily. To her chagrin, Jillian was standing over her. She must have fallen asleep right there at the table. She scrambled to sit up, feeling a slight sting in her cheek as the book page stuck to it peeled away.

"You've done enough for today. Time to go home," Jillian said gently.

"Always sending me home," Kelly mumbled, rubbing at the crick in her neck.

Jillian chuckled. "You'll be back here soon enough. Your day starts in eight hours."

Kelly groaned. "Goody."

"Come on," Jillian said, heaving her to her feet. Kelly realized it was the first time she'd touched her since they'd met again this morning. Jillian hesitated, then pulled something out of her purse. "Here, take this. It's the best concealer ever. It'll cover that spot on your neck."

"Thanks," Kelly said, taking the tube of makeup from Jillian's outstretched hand. "I'll see you tomorrow. Or later today, I guess. Good night."

CHAPTER FOUR

To Jillian's relief, other than her one sleepy reference to Jillian sending her home, Kelly made no allusions to their night together. She was pleasantly surprised that Kelly showed no inclination to coast on her famous name, either. In fact, she was proving to be one of the hardest workers Jillian had come across. When Jillian marked up her reports in red ink, Kelly accepted the feedback without complaint and never made the same mistake again. She sat in on several interviews and client meetings without making a peep, and her note-taking improved so much that Jillian couldn't find anything to criticize.

The first time Jillian complimented her work, Kelly turned pink with pleasure and stuttered for a minute afterward. Jillian remembered her reaction to praise at the bar and in bed. Kelly had tried to hide it, but it had shown on her face clear as day. Jillian had an urge to test her theory, to see how quickly she could turn Kelly into a flustered mess. She was instantly horrified with herself, giving herself a hard mental slap. She avoided Kelly for the rest of the day, sending her to the library even though she could have used her help on a more urgent case.

The plaintiff in the advertising copyright lawsuit dropped the case at the end of the week, and Jillian let Kelly leave at the relatively luxurious hour of eight on Friday to celebrate. When Jillian showed no signs of getting ready to go herself, Kelly paused in the doorway.

"Are you planning to leave at some point?" she asked tentatively.

Jillian gave her a wry smile. "Do you know what they say about making partner? It's like winning a pie-eating contest and finding out the prize is more pie."

Kelly furrowed her brow. "Meaning…"

"Meaning it never stops. Once you're a partner, every hour that isn't billed to a client is an hour wasted, including sleep," Jillian said. She was only half joking. She wondered if there was some magic number of billable hours or bank account balance she could hit that would finally be enough, if she would ever feel secure enough to take her foot off the gas.

Tessa certainly hadn't thought so, had blamed Jillian's work obsession for the collapse of their marriage. Jillian thought it was awfully convenient for all the blame to land on her shoulders, but what did it matter anyway now that the dust had settled? She was free to work as much as she wanted to now, and Tessa was free to move the violinist she'd supposedly just met into the house they'd once shared.

She realized Kelly was watching her expectantly from the doorway. Shit. Had she spoken? "Sorry, I was lost in thought there. Did you say something?"

"Just that you, um, that you should take some time for yourself too. You work really hard," Kelly said, coloring slightly and biting her lip.

God, she really was beautiful. Once again, Jillian found herself thinking of Sunday night, despite her best intentions. She wanted to point out that the last time she'd done something for herself, it hadn't gone so great in the long run. She forced the impulse aside. She was the one who'd insisted on acting like it had never happened. Kelly had been good about respecting that, and Jillian needed to be too.

"You don't have to worry about me," Jillian said firmly. "You can't count on many more opportunities like this. In your first year, at least. Go out, get drunk, have fun."

Kelly snorted. "More like do laundry and go to bed as soon as humanly possible. Besides, aren't we meeting with that new pro bono client first thing on Monday? I need to get the background research done."

Jillian couldn't help smiling. Kelly really was relentless, she had to give her that. "Okay, well, enjoy your laundry and research. See you Monday."

Kelly smiled shyly back at her and finally left.

❖

Jillian spent most of Saturday at the office, catching up on work she hadn't been able to do because of the time she'd been spending training Kelly. It was freeing to be able to work as many weekend hours as she wanted without having to worry about Tessa's reaction, but the thought of only the empty apartment waiting for her was depressing. She hadn't started thinking of it as *home* yet, and she wasn't sure she ever would. It still stung that Tessa had gotten the house, but she supposed it was only fair. She had picked it out, but Tessa had been the one to spend countless hours decorating it with carefully curated mementos from their travels. If Tessa had moved out with all of them, the house probably wouldn't feel like any more of a home than the new apartment did.

The office was her one constant, the only change being the empty spot on her desk where a picture of Tessa had once sat. She'd stay here all weekend if it weren't now associated with Kelly in her mind.

Even without Kelly around, she was never far from Jillian's thoughts. When Jillian moved on to the background material for their upcoming pro bono case, she kept thinking of Kelly, who might be reading the same document right now at home.

She wondered what branch of the Lattimores Kelly was from, one of the obscenely wealthy ones or a merely ridiculously wealthy one. She'd deliberately avoided any personal conversation during the past week. Between their history and the fact that Kelly would only be working for her for another week, she didn't see the point. It didn't mean she wasn't curious, though. Late in the afternoon, she opened Google and got as far as typing "Kelly Latt" before resolutely turning off her computer for the day.

She went to the gym in her apartment building instead, lifting weights and using the rowing machine before running on the treadmill until every muscle was aching and her lungs were frantically gasping for air. Finally, she was forced to stop, utterly exhausted. Her mind was still buzzing more than she'd like. Kelly had told her to take some time for herself. Maybe she was on to something.

She hauled herself up to her apartment and ran a bath. She found some fancy bath salts Elliot Springman's wife had given her at her bridal shower ten years ago. Why she had not only kept them for that long but moved them to the new place escaped her, but she shrugged and dumped some in. She poured a seltzer into a glass and set out her fanciest silk robe and softest slippers. She was about to step into the steaming water when she paused. It had been a long time since she'd taken some time for herself and certainly too long since she'd *taken time for herself*, wink-wink, nudge-nudge.

As soon as she opened the nightstand drawer, she knew she'd made a mistake. The strap-on and the pink vibrator she'd used on Kelly were right at the top. She'd actually been planning to use the pink, since it was both her favorite and waterproof, but for some reason, the sight of it made her a little sad. She resolutely pushed them aside and found another waterproof vibrator she didn't like nearly as much.

The first few minutes in the hot bath were blissful. The lavender scent from the bath salts was soothing, and she could feel her aching muscles starting to loosen up. The coldness of the seltzer and the carbonated bubbles on her tongue were a sensuous contrast to the hot smoothness of the water, and she realized she was ready to try out the inferior vibrator.

She let her mind wander. Almost immediately, her brain helpfully produced the memory of Kelly begging her to let her come. Well, fuck. This had been a bad idea from the start. She needed to pivot to something else or stop altogether. Those were the only reasonable courses of action.

The best case she could make for herself later was that she'd tried, she really had. She'd valiantly tried to turn her mind to half a dozen of her most reliable fantasies, but eventually, they'd all morphed into Kelly whispering, "I want you to wreck me," and spreading her legs for Jillian so eagerly. Finally, she gave in to the inevitable and let her body have what it wanted. The memory was embellished by smooth silk rope binding Kelly's hands securely to the headboard and Jillian's name on her lips as she came. A second later, Jillian herself was coming, the vibrator buried deep inside her and a hand clapped over her mouth to muffle her cries and any name she might have been about to say.

"Stupid, stupid, stupid," she chastised herself afterward. What had she been thinking? She hadn't, really. She'd been acting on pure instinct. She tried to look at it logically. The last sex she'd had had been with Kelly, so it was only natural that her mind might turn there. It was at the top of her mental drawer, so to speak, just like the vibrator and the strap-on. It didn't necessarily mean anything.

❖

When she heard Kelly greeting Ezra outside her office on Monday morning, Jillian schooled her face into the most blandly neutral look she could manage, even though her heart was thumping in her chest. By the time Kelly walked in a second later, she was pretty sure she looked normal.

"Good morning. I hope you got your laundry done because we have a busy week ahead of us. I started you off easy last week, but now, the real work begins," she said.

Kelly smiled nervously. "I was afraid you'd say something like that. Did you have a good weekend?"

Oh, fantastic. I used work as a replacement for human connection as usual, and I had a really great orgasm thinking about tying you up. "It was fine. Now that's enough chitchat. Let me see what you have on the pro bono case," Jillian said.

Kelly looked taken aback by the abruptness, but she pulled out the report she'd written over the weekend without another word. Jillian read it rapidly, impressed at the level of detail. Kelly had probably devoted her entire weekend to it. She'd figure out soon enough to save that level of dedication for billable work, but Jillian didn't have the heart to burst her idealistic bubble at this exact moment.

"This is the first time you're expected to speak in a client meeting," Jillian said. "I'll be taking the lead, of course, but this is a chance for you to start getting some practice in a lower stakes case."

"Lower stakes?" Kelly said incredulously. "That nursing home was abusing Alzheimer's patients and conning their families."

"Not lower stakes in terms of morality," Jillian said impatiently. "Of course I didn't mean that. But it usually costs two thousand dollars an hour for my time, and these families are getting it for free. That means they're getting a lot more work by a junior associate than a paying client would get. They still get free legal help, and you get to practice having face time with clients and handling a lot of aspects of the case yourself. It's a win-win."

Kelly pursed her lips like she wanted to push back but was thinking better of it. Jillian thought back to when she'd been a brand-new lawyer and tried to remember if she'd ever been this dedicated to pro bono work. It was hard to say with any accuracy, but she thought probably not. Instead, she'd been hungry to prove that she belonged in the Big Law boys' club, both to the partners and to herself. She'd worked more billable hours than any other associate but had to watch all her male colleagues get promoted first. Volunteer work had been at the bottom of her list of priorities.

Kelly, on the other hand, had the classic bleeding heart of youth. Jillian supposed that was one big advantage of being a Lattimore, too; the family prided itself on the many philanthropic endeavors of the Lattimore Foundation. Still, that usually ran along the lines of fancy fundraising galas and named university professorships, rather than boots-on-the-ground action. Kelly seemed to want to do more hands-on work. Jillian wondered if her heart was even in Big Law at all, or if she'd gone into it due to family pressure. She could have asked, but she reminded herself that she didn't care anyway, so why waste the time?

Ezra called to say the clients had arrived. They met with family members of some of the affected elderly patients and got enough information from them that Jillian was fairly sure they could at least get a lawsuit rolling. Whether they'd win it or not was another question. Kelly mostly acquitted herself well, but when one woman broke into tears about what had happened to her father, she veered off script.

"What happened to your dad is awful, but I promise, we can help you," Kelly said, gently squeezing the woman's hands.

Jillian stifled a groan. This was why junior associates weren't allowed to talk in most client meetings. As soon as the pro bono clients left, she snapped, "Never make promises to clients, *ever*. There are no guarantees, even when you think a case is a sure thing."

"Well, I had to say *something*," Kelly said defensively. "I get that I shouldn't have promised, but didn't you see how upset she was? She needed reassurance. And there was that case I found, it's in my report. Almost the exact same situation, and the jury awarded them millions in damages."

Jillian slapped her palms on her desk, and Kelly jumped in her seat. "And if Juror X had been on that jury instead of Juror Y, they would've lost. Or the judge excludes some key piece of evidence, and the whole case falls apart. You don't ever know what's going to happen. Clients need us to be calm and measured, not emotionally supportive."

Kelly stared at her mutinously. "What's wrong with having a little empathy? They need to at least know we care, and they weren't getting that from *you*."

"Go work for legal aid if you want to help every sad sack with legal problems," Jillian said scathingly. "But if you're going to stay here, you're going to need to grow a thicker skin."

"My skin is plenty thick," Kelly insisted. "You have no idea what I've—never mind, forget it."

Jillian took a deep breath. So much for being calm and measured herself. "Look," she said finally. "I know I sound harsh, but I really am trying to help you here. I see so much potential in you, but there are a lot of pitfalls in this business, especially for women. I want you to be the best lawyer you can be, and I think that's a damn good one."

"Thanks," Kelly said quietly. "I really do appreciate all you've been doing for me, especially given the… circumstances. I've learned more this past week than I did in most of law school."

Jillian gave her a small smile. "You're welcome."

Kelly smiled back, and Jillian forgot why she had been angry in the first place. She was on the brink of suggesting they take a quick breather and go to Starbucks together when her phone rang.

"There's someone named Dan asking for Kelly?" Ezra said. Kelly's face lit up when Jillian passed on the message, so Jillian had Ezra send him in.

A second later, a man about Kelly's age walked in. "Hi, Kell," he said brightly.

"Danny," Kelly cried, flinging her arms around him.

"I'm here for a meeting, but I got here early. I'm glad I caught you. I know the first few weeks are especially crazy," he said, smiling at her.

"Jillian, this is Dan Howell. He's in his second year at Simpson McClaskey. We, uh, went to Yale and Harvard Law together. Danny, this is Jillian Briggs," Kelly said, a slight flush on her face.

"That's a funny way of saying we dated for four years," Dan said with a grin. "Nice to meet you."

Jillian shook his outstretched hand. He was good-looking, she supposed, in a preppy kind of way, like Christopher Reeve in Clark Kent mode crossed with JFK. They'd probably met as neighbors while summering in Newport or something. She tried not to instantly hate him.

"I can spare you for fifteen minutes if you two want to go catch up," she said. *There. Look how magnanimous I am.*

Kelly beamed. "That'd be great! Thanks, Jillian. We'll just be in the break room if you want me back sooner."

She followed Dan out of the office and didn't look back once.

CHAPTER FIVE

"What's it like working for Jillian Briggs? Weren't you supposed to be with Leon Marsh?" Dan asked over coffee.

Kelly explained the temporary reassignment. "It's been great. She's super intimidating, but I'm learning a ton."

He nodded. "That's awesome. She's not exactly hard on the eyes, either. Most partners are old dudes with ear hair, but her..." He let out a low whistle.

"Don't be gross," she said, rolling her eyes. She felt a flare of possessiveness in her chest, although whether it was for Dan or Jillian, she didn't care to analyze.

"I didn't mean any disrespect. All I'm saying is she's a very attractive woman in addition to being a badass lawyer. You should hear the way they talk about her over at McClaskey. It's like she's the boogeyman or something. They're all terrified of her. I expected her to look more like Margaret Thatcher or maybe Jason Voorhees."

"I uh, hadn't noticed her looks," Kelly lied.

Dan raised his eyebrows. "If you say so," he said skeptically.

Her stomach dropped. She'd had occasion in the past to wonder if he suspected her interest in women wasn't always platonic. She hoped he hadn't picked up on anything between her and Jillian. Jillian had been doing a good job of keeping up the pretense that nothing had happened between them, but Kelly knew she was still ridiculously responsive to Jillian's attention.

She hurriedly changed the subject. "How's your family?" she asked.

"They're great," he said. "My mom asked about you just the other day, actually. She says hi. I think she keeps hoping we'll get back together."

"Tell her I say hi back." The Howells had always been kind and welcoming to her, and she genuinely missed them.

He paused, then said, "Listen, Kell…you might be seeing someone for all I know, but if you're not…my mom might not be the only one hoping for that."

She froze. How many times had she longed for this exact conversation in the year since their breakup? Now that it was actually happening, she felt decidedly ambivalent about it. Dan was a known quantity, kind and smart and funny. Maybe he didn't quite drive her wild with excitement, but that was only to be expected after being together for so long. She could easily picture slipping back into their comfortable and familiar relationship, his family happy, hers as close to happy as they ever were when it came to her.

Somehow, the picture didn't feel quite right anymore, though. Obviously, she didn't have a future with Jillian, but ever since their night together, she couldn't imagine going back to the way things had been before. Comfortable and familiar were no longer enough. She needed something more, even if she didn't yet know what that *more* was.

He knew her well enough to read it all on her face. "So that's a no, then?" he said.

"I'm sorry," she said. "I *want* to want to, it's just…"

"You met someone else."

"Yes and no. It wasn't anything serious. And I think it's only one-sided on my part anyway, but I just…can't right now."

He smiled sadly. "I really doubt it's just you. You're one of a kind, Kell. I hope it works out for you. And if it doesn't, whoever she is, she doesn't deserve you anyway."

"You're not going to tell anyone, are you?" she asked urgently. Of course he had seen right through her, although thankfully, he hadn't connected the dots to Jillian. "My family…"

"Of course not. I'm not a monster," he said indignantly.

She squeezed his hands across the table. "I know, I just had to be sure. Thanks. You're a really good friend."

There wasn't much more to say after that, and their fifteen minutes were almost up anyway, so they said good-bye. Even as he walked away, she wondered if she'd made the right choice.

"Have fun?" Jillian asked, barely glancing up when Kelly reentered her office.

"I guess," Kelly said, not sure how to process what had just happened.

Jillian finally looked at her, perhaps hearing something off in her voice. "Are you okay?"

Jillian had made it clear she wasn't interested in hearing about anything personal from her, so at first Kelly just nodded. Jillian looked like she was about to say something, but some insanity came over Kelly, and she spoke first. "He asked about getting back together," she blurted out.

Jillian's face was an expressionless mask. "It can be hard to balance a relationship with this career, but there's something to be said for being with someone who knows the demands of the job."

Kelly opened her mouth to say that she'd already turned him down, but what if Jillian asked why? She certainly didn't want to risk getting into her complicated feelings about her. Instead, she asked "So you think I should?"

Jillian scoffed. "As you may recall, I just got divorced ten days ago, so I'm definitely not the person to ask for relationship advice. But I will say that my workload was a contributing factor. Or the primary factor, if you ask Tessa."

"Sorry, I know this isn't work-related. What case are we working on now?" Kelly asked. She didn't want to test Jillian's patience, and this was getting close to dangerous conversational territory anyway. Jillian had already let slip more about her past relationship than Kelly had heard before, and it probably wouldn't be long before she regretted opening up that much.

❖

They spent most of the week preparing their defense in a copyright infringement case for the local minor-league baseball team, although Kelly stayed late every day to work on the pro bono case. She and Jillian reached a detente on the subject, and Jillian no longer tried to dissuade her from doing pro bono work as long as she did it on her own time. She found it invigorating, even as the lack of sleep was starting to catch up with her. It certainly felt more meaningful than how many billable hours they could tack on to the baseball case.

Jillian, on the other hand, was in her element. Intellectual property was her favorite area of law, and the bigger the case, the happier she seemed to be. Kelly told her what Dan had said about her reputation at his firm, and Jillian rubbed her hands together in glee. "There's nothing I love more than terrifying grown men," she said smugly, and Kelly giggled.

She could hardly believe that her time working for Jillian was almost up. As awkward as it had been at times, she found herself dreading coming in on Monday and not seeing Jillian. She wondered if Jillian still intended to stick to the original plan of never working together again, but she didn't quite dare ask.

On Thursday, they were welcoming a delegation from the baseball team to officially sign the paperwork. Kelly was feeling confident as she marched with Jillian to the same conference room as the deposition from her first day.

There were so many people there that she didn't see Sarah at first. In fact, it was only when one of the baseball team owners, Tim, did a double take at seeing Kelly and said, "What on earth?" that she realized Sarah was there.

A blond head at the back of the room turned, and Kelly groaned internally. It wasn't quite like looking in a mirror; Sarah's face was a little longer, her nose a little narrower, and she wore her hair parted in the middle instead of to the side. They were still similar enough that Tim had spotted it, and so had Jillian. Her eyes flicked rapidly between them.

Sarah finally noticed, and her amiable smile turned into the sneer of distaste she usually wore in Kelly's presence. Kelly froze on the spot, and she could feel Jillian watching her closely.

"We seem to have some doppelgangers," Tim said affably, either oblivious to the sudden tension in the room or trying to smooth it over. "Do you two know each other?"

Sarah whispered something to the man next to her, and

soon, he too was staring daggers. She showed no inclination to answer Tim's question.

"We're...sisters," Kelly said.

"*Half* sisters," Sarah interjected.

Kelly wasn't surprised by the correction. She even wondered if subconsciously, she'd set Sarah up just to see if she'd do it in front of this group of people. Of course she would. She'd never pass up a chance to try to remind Kelly just how much she resented her very existence.

"Well, I guess no introductions are needed," Tim said, chuckling.

Jillian had gone very still, and Kelly could practically hear the cogs in her brain turning. "I know the rest of you, but I don't believe we've met," she said to Sarah in her most inoffensive tone. "I'm Jillian Briggs, a partner here and Kelly's boss at the moment."

Sarah eyed Jillian like she was looking for a reason to be offended, but apparently, she found none. "Sarah Lattimore," she said, shaking Jillian's outstretched hand briefly. "And this is my fiancé, Ted Richmond."

Fiancé? Kelly hadn't known she was even dating anyone, but then again, she wasn't exactly at the top of Sarah's Christmas card list. That explained what she was doing here, though: Ted was a minority share owner of the team. She hoped their connection was distant enough not to be considered a conflict of interest. A first-year associate losing the firm this big a client would earn a permanent black mark in their record.

Jillian certainly didn't need to remind Kelly not to talk in this meeting. She was too focused on trying not to turn red under the weight of Sarah's and Ted's stares. At one point, Jillian glanced at her out of the corner of her eye. A second later, she felt Jillian's hand on her knee. There was nothing sexual about the gesture; instead, Jillian gave it a gentle squeeze and removed her hand. Kelly felt bolstered enough to meet Sarah's eyes across the table. She smiled blandly, and to her amazement, Sarah colored slightly and looked away first.

Sarah and Ted swept out of the conference room before the ink was even dry on the contracts without a word to either Kelly or Jillian. Jillian kept up a running monologue about the baseball litigation as they returned to her office. She stopped off at Ezra's desk and told him to hold her calls before ushering Kelly inside.

Instead of sitting at the desk, Jillian led her over to the couch and armchairs where she often met with clients. She sat Kelly on the couch and took an armchair for herself.

"Do you want to talk about it?" she asked quietly.

Kelly exhaled tremulously. She was proud of herself for keeping it together in front of Sarah, but the unexpected encounter had really thrown her. She didn't want to dump all her messy family drama on Jillian, but on the other hand, Jillian was wearing an expression Kelly had never seen on her face before, inviting but undemanding. Whether she chose to open up or not, she knew Jillian would respect it. She opened her mouth several times, not sure how to start.

"Sarah and I have the same father," she said at last, "but different mothers. She's two years older than me. He had an affair with my mom for years. It almost ruined Sarah's parents' marriage when her mom found out about it. I guess it kind of did in a way. They stayed married, but from what I hear, they still fight about it all the time. That's why she hates me so much. Also because it was a big scandal at the time, at least among the Lattimores. They managed to keep it pretty quiet outside the family."

Jillian nodded for her to continue.

"I didn't realize there was something weird about my family until I was maybe seven or eight. My mom tried to make it as normal as she could, but my dad was hardly ever around. There were other kids whose parents didn't live together, but their dads wouldn't avoid taking pictures with them or suddenly duck out of their birthday parties if they saw someone they knew." She stared at her hands, fingers threaded together in her lap.

"Eventually, Sarah's mom found out when I was nine. She showed up at our house, and it was a whole big scene. On my birthday, no less. After that, everything got worse. I didn't see my dad again for years. He'd been giving my mom money, but he cut her off to appease his wife. We had to move to this tiny apartment, and our only income was the court-ordered child support payments. Sometimes, his parents would pay for stuff for me, but only if they were feeling generous, so we always had to suck up to them and stay on their good side. Both of my mom's parents died before I was born, so they were the only grandparents I had. I just wanted them to like me, you know?"

To her embarrassment, she felt tears starting to form. She'd never told the whole story like this, all in one go. Even Dan had learned her history piece by piece, over the course of months. Jillian reached over and gave her hand a light squeeze, then handed her a tissue.

"No matter what I did, it was never enough. They'd only pay for me to do the activities Sarah did, but they'd always compare us. It was always 'Sarah this' and 'Sarah that.' It was like they wanted to pit us against each other. The only thing I ever did that they didn't want me to was apply to Yale because Sarah was going there. After I got in, they refused to pay for it."

"Wow," Jillian said softly. "This is soap opera worthy. It can't have been fun to live it."

Kelly shrugged. "I don't want to make it sound worse than it was. I always had a roof over my head and enough to eat and a mom who loved me. She definitely made some questionable choices in her personal life, but she's always been a good mom."

Jillian nodded. "So what happened next? You went to Yale, so did they change their minds about paying for it?"

"No, they did not," Kelly said ruefully. "I talked to my dad for the first time in nine years to ask him. He said he wanted to, but he was afraid his wife or his parents would find out."

Jillian snorted. "What a pussy. I'm sorry, I know he's your dad and all, but he kind of sucks."

Amazingly, Kelly felt a laugh bubble up in her chest. It escaped as more of a strangled choking noise, but the fact that she wanted to laugh at all while talking about this was a surprise. She figured she might as well finish the story now that she'd gotten this far. "Anyway, I didn't get any financial aid from the school because they look at both your parents' incomes, and obviously, no Lattimore is going to qualify for aid. I took out some loans, and I applied for every merit-based scholarship I could find. Some of them were only for, like, a hundred dollars, but I applied to literally hundreds, and that all added up. I also worked about twenty hours a week, so I only had about ten thousand dollars in debt from undergrad."

"And you still managed to graduate summa cum laude, as I recall," Jillian said.

"Yep," Kelly said proudly. She was touched that Jillian remembered. "And Sarah had only gotten magna cum laude, so that was kind of the nail in the coffin for us having any kind of a relationship."

"That must have really steamed her clams," Jillian said gleefully.

Kelly smiled, but she couldn't fully share in Jillian's delight. "I don't really blame her for not liking me. I'm sure it didn't make her childhood great either. And I could've gone to a different school."

"Don't you dare take any of the blame for this," Jillian said sternly. "Come on, it's *Yale*. What were you going to do, not go?"

"I don't regret it," Kelly admitted. "I loved it there. I made some great friends, I met Dan there…"

The only reason she noticed the slight shadow cross Jillian's face was her obsessive mental cataloging of Jillian's expressions. It baffled her. Jillian had seemed interested in the story up to now, and it was obviously almost done. She hurried to wrap it up.

"Law school's a different story. I still owe about three hundred thousand for that, which is why I took this job. But when I told my grandparents I'd be working here, they were so proud. My mom is hoping they'll offer to pay off my loans. My dad even called to congratulate me. I guess he didn't tell Sarah, or she probably wouldn't have come today," she said.

Jillian rolled her eyes. "There's that classic 'Kelly's dad' move. Which one is your dad, by the way?"

"Benton Lattimore."

"Well, from now on, 'pulling a Benton' is going to be in my vocabulary for when someone folds like a cheap suit."

Kelly giggled. "Hopefully, you won't need it much."

"Not for myself, anyway," Jillian said, crossing her fingers. She sighed heavily. "You've had a hell of an afternoon. You know what you need now?"

Kelly's immediate answer to that was decidedly not work appropriate, so she mutely shook her head.

"A fuckton of carbs," Jillian said. "Let's go."

CHAPTER SIX

A s soon as they sat in the restaurant, Jillian regretted her choice. For one thing, there was something unavoidably date-like about sitting across a tiny candlelit table from someone she'd both slept with and spent most of her waking hours with over the last two weeks. For another, she'd picked this place forgetting that it had been one of Tessa's favorites. Memories, both good and bad, bombarded her from every angle.

She thought about everything Kelly had told her that afternoon. It hadn't been what she'd expected at all. What must that have been like for Kelly, growing up with the vast majority of her family being ashamed of her very existence? Whatever Kelly said in their defense, Jillian had plenty of blame to spare for Sarah, Benton, and all the other Lattimores. It infuriated her to think of Kelly laboring away in a job she didn't even like to pay off loans her father could have easily covered without noticing the drop in his bank account. Benton Lattimore had better hope he never ran into Jillian around town because she would have some choice words for the man.

Either Kelly was the most scrupulous menu reader on earth or she was feeling self-conscious about how much personal information she'd shared today because she hadn't looked up since they'd sat down. It gave Jillian a chance to study her face, something she couldn't usually do without the risk of being observed. She found herself transfixed by a tiny beauty mark below Kelly's left eye. How had she never noticed it before?

"What's good here?" Kelly asked quietly, finally looking up.

Jillian wrenched her gaze away and tried to act like she hadn't just been staring. "I've never had a bad meal here, but my favorite is the carbonara. They make all their own pasta in-house."

She recognized their server from some of her many visits here with Tessa. He glanced between her and Kelly with his eyebrows raised but thankfully didn't say anything when he dropped off a plate of focaccia and took their order.

"Could you bring us some more bread?" Jillian asked before he left.

He looked at the bread he'd just delivered. "You mean more than this?"

She gave him an icy stare. "I think I was very clear."

He scurried away, looking chastened. Kelly raised an eyebrow.

"Oh, don't look at me like that," Jillian said. "I always tip thirty percent, and he knows it."

Kelly laughed, then said, "I'm sorry I dumped all of that on you."

"Don't be silly. I asked. I'm sorry I made so many assumptions about you just because of your last name. I feel like a bit of an asshole now."

"Well, you know what they say about when you assume…"

Jillian rolled her eyes but couldn't hold in her laugh. "Yeah, yeah."

Kelly took a bite of bread, and her eyes lit up. "Oh man,

this is delicious. I usually try not to eat a lot of bread, but this is so good."

"This is a meal free of limits or judgment," Jillian said. "When I said a fuckton of carbs, I *meant* a fuckton of carbs. We're also getting dessert, and don't try to argue with me."

"I wouldn't even if I wanted to," Kelly assured her. "I wouldn't dare go up against Margaret Jason Thatcher Voorhees, Esquire."

Jillian snorted. "Your Dan is pretty funny, I have to give him that."

Kelly paused for a beat, then said, "You know basically my whole life story now, but I don't really know that much about you at all. How'd you end up becoming a lawyer?"

"Oh, that kind of happened by accident," Jillian said. "I grew up in a little town on a lake in New Hampshire. There was this old guy, Jerome, who was the town outcast. He was a bit of a hoarder and kind of a Boo Radley type, you know? I…didn't have a great time in high school. I hadn't come out yet or anything, but the other kids could tell I was different, and I got bullied a lot. Anyway, I'd go to Jerome's house after school most days, do my homework, listen to his stories from World War Two…"

"I need this story to have a happy ending," Kelly said.

"No spoilers. The whole region would get flooded with obnoxious rich city people in the summer. Some of them were probably your third cousins or something, now that I think about it. Jerome had the best plot of land on the whole lake, tons of waterfront property. Developers were offering him ten times what it was worth, but he wouldn't sell. Finally, they started playing the legal game—filing lawsuits and public nuisance complaints and so on—to try to get his place condemned. He couldn't afford a lawyer, so every weekend, we'd drive down to the state law library in Concord and look up every property rights case, state statute, and town ordinance we could find. He had to represent himself in court ten times, but he won every time, and eventually, they gave up. I think they figured he was old anyway, and they'd snap it up when he died. He didn't have any family, so it would've gone up for auction."

"You said 'would've,'" Kelly said, looking rapt. "What actually happened?"

"Well," Jillian said, trying and failing to keep the smugness out of her voice. "In one of their attempts to force him out, they'd bribed the town council to pass a massive property tax hike based on waterfront footage. They figured he'd never be able to afford it. During our research, I found a loophole. He was able to divide his property, keep about fifty feet of lakeshore for himself, and he donated the rest of it to the state university for ecology research. The university is tax-exempt, so even with the tax increase on the land he kept, they lost a ton of money, and now, it can never be developed."

"That's *awesome,*" Kelly said. "What a baller move."

Jillian laughed. "It was. He mostly just wanted to stick it to the developers and the town, but it's really a beautiful spot, and the lake is much nicer and calmer for it. I got such a rush from it all that I never even considered being anything but a lawyer."

"What happened to his house and the land he kept? Is he still alive?"

Jillian shook her head. "No, he died about fifteen years ago. He actually left the rest of his property to me."

Kelly stared at her, agog. "That's the dream, right? Some eccentric old person adopts you and leaves you their estate?"

"Ha. It's hardly what I'd call an estate. The house is only about three hundred square feet, and the plumbing is temperamental at best. But seriously, it was a wonderful surprise. For all the time we spent together, we never really talked that much. Jerome preferred to communicate mostly in monosyllables."

"But he could tell you needed a safe haven," Kelly mused. "I'm really sorry you got bullied in high school. That's awful."

"I hope things have gotten better since then," Jillian said. "What about for you? Were you out in high school?"

Kelly flushed slightly. "No. Actually…" She paused as their server cleared their dinner plates. After he left, she continued, "I, uh, I guess I'm not technically *out* now. At least not to anyone in my family. I haven't really…*you're* actually the only, um, woman I've ever been with." Her face was decidedly red now, and she avoided Jillian's eyes.

Jillian felt her eyes widen in shock, but thankfully, Kelly didn't notice. She was still staring determinedly at her lap like it held all the secrets of the universe. Sure, Jillian had picked up that Kelly wasn't exactly a regular on the gay club scene, but this was still a surprise. She wondered if she would have done anything differently that night in the club if she'd known or afterward in her apartment. More importantly, she wondered if she *should* have, like, maybe left Kelly alone to have a gentler introduction to it all.

Kelly finally looked up, although her gaze was slightly over Jillian's shoulder. "I hope you're not upset or anything, and it wasn't, like, a faux pas not to mention it—"

"Everyone figures this stuff out in their own time," Jillian interrupted. "Don't even worry about it."

Kelly shrugged. "I hardly tell my grandparents anything about my personal life. I told them when Dan and I got together because they have a house near his grandparents' on the Cape, and they knew each other, but that's about it. I don't really know how they'd react if I came out, honestly. I'd like to think they wouldn't care, but at the same time, they're pretty old-school, and…" She trailed off.

"You just never know?" Jillian suggested. She supposed there wouldn't be any need for Kelly to come out to them anyway if she and Dan were getting back together. Sure, it had been the Cape and not Newport, but she'd still have called that from a mile away. She didn't feel a rush of satisfaction at the correct guess the way she usually would have, though.

"Right," Kelly said with a small smile. "And that's kind of why I haven't told my mom, either. Not because of how she'd feel personally, but I know she'd just worry about my grandparents being upset."

"You spend an awful lot of time worrying about how everyone else feels," Jillian observed.

Kelly blinked at her. "I guess you're right. I never thought about it that way before."

"Some free advice? I'm not saying you should be a selfish asshole like me, but you should look out for your own happiness because no one else will."

"You're not a selfish asshole," Kelly said indignantly.

Jillian smiled indulgently. "I think my ex-wife would disagree with you there, but that's very kind of you to say."

"It's not like she's an objective observer," Kelly pointed out. "If you asked Sarah, I'm sure she'd say all sorts of things about me that aren't particularly nice, but that doesn't mean they're true. Speaking of which, do you think it'll be a problem for the case to have me working on it, given my connection with Sarah and Ted? Do we need to head back?"

"No, we've got plenty of time." Instinctively, Jillian had glanced at her watch to note the second they'd started talking about the case. "Just keeping track for billing purposes. You asked about the potential conflict of interest. Do you think you can work on this case in a fair and unbiased manner? Make sure you take at least thirty seconds to answer."

Kelly furrowed her brow in confusion for a second before

she understood what Jillian meant. "So we hit a full minute talking about the case and can bill for it."

"Because?" Jillian prompted.

"We bill in tenth of an hour increments, so one minute rounds up to six," Kelly said, rolling her eyes.

"Bingo." Even if Kelly wasn't going to stay at the firm, Leon would expect her to keep an eye on such things as long she was working for him. She might as well get the habit ingrained in her now.

"So this two-minute conversation is going to cost them… let's see, two hundred and fifty dollars between the two of us. You know, bill padding is one of the many things I don't like about Big Law."

"Most of our clients can afford to use hundred-dollar bills as toilet paper, including Ted, so it's not keeping me up at night. You haven't answered my initial question, by the way."

Kelly pressed her chin to the back of her hand as she considered. "I won't deny that the idea of getting to Sarah in some way appeals to me, but this would be so indirect that it wouldn't even really count. And I don't think revenge is usually as satisfying as you think it's going to be. Plus, legal malpractice isn't something to mess around with. I don't want to be disbarred over a family feud."

Jillian nodded, impressed at Kelly's emotional restraint. "I don't think it's a close enough relationship to be a problem, personally. It'd be best to keep you out of future client meetings to avoid any further awkwardness, but I'd prefer to have your help on the background work unless Ted or one of the other owners objects. Technically, Sarah herself doesn't have any say."

"I'm glad we agree," Kelly said with a relieved smile. "Did I talk long enough?"

Jillian laughed as she checked her watch again. "Yes, we're golden. We definitely didn't talk about the case enough to bill this as a working dinner, though."

She insisted on picking up the check, shouting down Kelly's protests. Belatedly, she realized it increased the date-like feeling of the evening. Then again, she wouldn't normally bring up her ex on a date. Besides, it just made sense for her to pay. It was common enough for partners to treat their associates now and then, and coming here had been her idea. It would be a bad look if anyone from the firm found out about their night together, but they'd gotten this far keeping it under wraps.

It took them quite a while to get anything done once they were back in the office. The carb binge, while delicious, left them both sleepy and yawning. Jillian let Kelly take a twenty-minute catnap on the couch while she guzzled coffee and caught up on emails. She knew they were in for another late night after their lengthy dinner break, but she'd never minded the long hours of the job, and she and Kelly only had one more day together anyway. They might as well get as much done as they could before she was back to her lone wolf status quo. Kelly had proved remarkably competent for a brand-new associate, and she'd miss having her help. Leon was a lucky son of a bitch.

By the time midnight rolled around, they were both feeling a little punchy, and Jillian nearly jumped out of her chair as Kelly let out a snort of laughter. "What's so funny over there?" she asked.

"You have to read this. I can't even..." Kelly trailed off into uncontrollable giggles as Jillian joined her on the couch.

The client for their current case was a film studio that made low-budget horror movies, and in the course of her research, Kelly had come across user-submitted reviews of some of the movies. While a few were surprisingly thoughtful, the majority could best be described as rambling screeds. They took turns reading the most unhinged ones aloud, cackling with laughter.

"'This might be the greatest film ever made since *Schindler's List*,'" Jillian read.

Kelly snickered. "Obviously. It goes *Casablanca*, *Schindler's List*, then *Lake Bloodshed Part 4: Bob's Revenge*."

"What the hell kind of name is Bob for a slasher, anyway? Not even Bobby? You need that second syllable. Jason, Freddy, Michael…Bob doesn't sound scary at all. And even calling it a 'film' is a bit rich," Jillian said, shaking her head.

The reviews went downhill from there. When Kelly started laughing too hard to speak, Jillian kicked off her shoes and folded her legs up on the couch, leaning close to read off her computer screen. She could feel the warmth of Kelly's body next to hers, and she vaguely thought that this had not, perhaps, been one of her brighter ideas. Their eyes met, and their laughter died away. Time stood still, and Jillian was pretty sure she no longer remembered how to breathe. Kelly bit her lip, and Jillian couldn't stop staring at her mouth. Kelly hesitated, then leaned forward and kissed her.

Jillian sat frozen for a beat, and then her mind shut off, and she was returning the kiss with a fervor that shocked her. Kelly buried a hand in Jillian's hair and gasped as Jillian nipped at her lip and dropped a hand to her waist to pull her close. Kelly moaned and pressed their bodies together when Jillian's tongue slipped into her mouth. Desire swirled in Jillian's gut as they clutched at each other feverishly. She pushed Kelly onto her back, pinning her to the couch. Kelly grabbed her ass as she ground her hips up against Jillian's, whimpering with pleasure.

The sound finally triggered a synapse in Jillian's brain,

and she pulled away, her breathing heavy. "Wait," she panted. "We can't do this."

Kelly stared up at her, her cheeks flushed and her lips pink and swollen. "Right," she said dazedly. "But what if we did anyway?"

Jillian forced herself to sit up fully and move to the end of the couch so they were no longer touching. "No. No, no, no." The shock was wearing off, and she was starting to freak out a little. Almost sleeping with a junior associate? Iffy at best. Almost sleeping with one she was actively supervising right here in her office? Reckless to the point of insanity. One word to the wrong person could bring everything she'd been working for over the last twenty years crashing to the ground and leave her reputation in tatters. It certainly wouldn't do Kelly's career any good either, not to mention her rekindled relationship with Dan.

She surged to her feet and scooped up her shoes without bothering to put them on, then grabbed her purse and phone off the desk and bolted.

Okay, maybe she was freaking out more than a little.

CHAPTER SEVEN

Kelly was so stunned by the abruptness of Jillian's departure that all she could do was sit on the couch for several minutes and try to will her head to stop spinning. The whole day felt like a fever dream, from the surprise run-in with Sarah to spilling her guts to Jillian to their definitely-not-a-date dinner. The mind meltingly hot make-out session was just the icing on the cake.

Not that there was anything else about it she would describe as *just*. Even through the brain fog, she could tell she was still embarrassingly turned on after only a few simple touches from Jillian. She knew Jillian was right and hooking up tonight would have been a mistake, but right now, her body was insisting the only mistake they'd made was stopping.

She barely slept that night, too busy worrying about what would happen in the morning. She'd really thought it was all in her head, that she was projecting her own desire for Jillian onto something that wasn't there. Once Kelly had made the first move, though, Jillian had *gone for it* as avidly as she had that night in her apartment. She was under no delusions that Jillian was interested in dating her; she'd been clear about that from almost the moment they'd met, and why would she be, anyway? But at least the physical attraction was still there on both sides, even if they couldn't act on it right now.

Trepidation flooded her veins as she got to work on Friday. She wondered if Jillian would bother addressing what they'd done the night before or skip ahead to the part where they pretended it hadn't happened. When she reached Ezra's desk, though, he stopped her before she could enter Jillian's office.

"Good morning," he said with an apologetic smile. "Ms. Briggs is in some highly sensitive meetings all day, so she asked me to send you over to Mr. Marsh's office and have a senior associate get you started on one of his cases."

Kelly's stomach dropped. "But it's our last day together. I didn't finish the research for the horror movie lawsuit, and she was going to help me with a motion for the nursing home case…"

There was real regret on Ezra's face as he said, "I know, and I'm sorry. If you draft the motion, I'll make sure she reviews it ASAP." He stood. "Come on, I'll show you where to go. At least you'll have a jump-start for Monday when Mr. Marsh is back, and you'll have your own office now."

Numbly, Kelly trailed behind him as they wove their way across the busy maze of offices and cubicles, but her mind was back in Jillian's office. This had to be connected to last night, right? She'd been excluded from a few client meetings Jillian deemed too important and top secret, but never for an entire day. They'd even had a game plan for what they were going to work on today. If she could just talk to Jillian, reassure her that she wasn't upset and wasn't going to say anything…

"Ezra? Can you squeeze me in for just five minutes with her sometime today?" she asked, trying not to sound desperate.

He winced and avoided meeting her eyes. "I'm sorry. I'd

really like to help you out, but she told me not…I mean, that she'd be unavailable all day."

She sighed. Apparently, Jillian was shutting her out altogether, both literally and figuratively.

Ezra studied her, then said, "Look. I don't know what's going on with her, but whatever it is, I'm sure it's nothing personal. She really likes you. I've never seen her take to a new associate like this before."

Oh, it's definitely personal. But at least I'm not just one in a long line of conquests, I guess. "Thanks," she told Ezra. "I liked working for her. I'm…I'm going to miss her and you too."

"Same. And if you need anything, I'm just across the way," he said with a smile and left her to it.

Indeed, she could see both his workstation and the door to Jillian's office from her tiny, glass-walled office on the other side of the floor. She tried to focus on her work, but every few minutes, she found herself watching for any sign of Jillian. Unfortunately, Jillian was set up well for a long siege. She had her own bathroom in her office and Ezra to bring her meals. There was no need for her to leave unless she had a meeting elsewhere in the building, which apparently, she didn't today. The only time the door opened that Kelly saw was when Ezra delivered a salad in the afternoon.

Her concentration wasn't helped by the case she was working on. Greg, a senior associate who reported to Leon, wanted her help preparing the defense for an accountant who was being sued by his former clients for running a Ponzi scheme. The accountant came across as a real jerk, and the case wasn't even interesting legal work on an academic level. At least the horror movie suit was fun, and her pro bono work was contributing something of value to the world.

She reminded herself that if she kept saving scrupulously

and stuck it out here, she could pay off her loans in eight years, maybe seven, depending on bonuses. Then, she'd be free to do the kind of law she really wanted to do and help the people who needed it most. The trouble was, sticking it out had seemed a lot more bearable when she was working for Jillian. Greg seemed nice enough, but when the conversation strayed from work, they had little in common to talk about.

She spent the weekend working on the nursing home case and emailed Jillian the finished draft of her motion late Saturday night. Jillian replied within minutes, the document marked up with feedback but the body of the email blank except for her automatic signature.

❖

On Sunday, Kelly had lunch with her friend Allison and filled her in on almost everything that had happened, although she kept her word and didn't mention the night in Jillian's apartment. It was hard to believe that was only two weeks ago. It felt like a lifetime. The rest of it was juicy enough on its own for Allison, though.

"She kissed you? I can't *believe* she kissed you," Allison exclaimed, dropping her fork onto her empty salad plate. "That's kind of uncool but also kind of hot."

"No, she just kissed me back after *I* kissed *her,*" Kelly corrected. "And then she stopped it before anything else could happen."

Allison raised her eyebrows as she said, "You sound disappointed."

Kelly could feel herself blushing. "I mean, I get why she did. I just wish she wasn't avoiding me now."

"Maybe she's just waiting until tomorrow when she's not your boss anymore to ask you out," Allison said encouragingly.

Hope flared briefly in Kelly's chest, but reality set in immediately, and she shook her head. "No, I really don't think so. She just got divorced. At best I'd be a rebound fling."

"Too bad," Allison said. "Now I feel invested in this."

"Oh well," Kelly said with a sigh. "Enough about that. What's new with you?"

They spent the rest of lunch going through Allison's run of bad Tinder dates and then stalking some of their old college classmates on social media, but part of Kelly's brain stayed stuck on Jillian. As improbable as it was, she couldn't help hoping Allison was on to something.

Although Allison had been overly optimistic, Jillian had at least thawed a little by Monday. Their eyes met when Jillian was leaving her office for a meeting, and she gave Kelly a polite wave. Kelly looked to either side to make sure Jillian was actually waving at her. Jillian laughed and nodded, so she waved back. It was a tiny interaction, but it was enough to fuel her mood throughout the day.

She needed the boost, as it turned out. Leon was frustrating to work for, giving her vague directions and then sending her work back to be revised endlessly. It seemed like he didn't know what he wanted, but he definitely knew what he *didn't* want.

Greg gave her a commiserating smile, but his only advice was, "Just think about the paycheck and do what he tells you."

Late in the day, after the support staff and a lot of the other lawyers had gone home, Leon came storming out of his office as angrily as he could on crutches. He slammed something down on her desk. "What the hell is this?" he barked.

She looked at it. "Um, it's a motion for discovery?" she said cautiously.

"Who told you to write it this way? Are you *trying* to make me look like an idiot?" he yelled.

She opened her mouth to respond but wasn't sure where to begin. Maybe it hadn't been her best work, but he'd changed his mind about it five times already. He was glaring, and she knew she needed to say something.

"You don't need help from anyone else for that, Leon," a familiar voice said. Jillian had walked over without either of them noticing and was now scanning the draft she'd plucked off Kelly's desk. She snorted when she finished, noticing all the strike-throughs and revisions.

He glared at Jillian. "I suppose this is your influence, huh?"

She raised her eyebrows innocently. "What is? Teaching her to write a motion for discovery so you'll get actual evidence instead of a vague fishing expedition that any judge would throw out in ten seconds? She already knew how to do that, but I'm happy to take some of the credit too."

"Don't start with me, Jillian, I have a lot of work to do—" he started, but she cut him off.

"Then maybe you should actually *do your work* instead of screaming at your associate for doing hers," she snapped.

Leon gaped at her, apparently lost for words. Jillian gave him her coldest stare until he retreated to his office.

"Thanks," Kelly said quietly.

"Don't mention it," Jillian said, smiling gently. "I can't stand bullies. You couldn't get away with mouthing off to him, but I can. In fact, I thrive on it. It's a good way to let off steam."

Kelly giggled. "Some people do yoga, some jog, and you needle Leon?"

Jillian nodded ruefully. "It's probably not the healthiest thing for me, either, but I think we both know I don't always make great choices."

Kelly's breath caught. Were they actually going to talk about it now?

"Anyway, I'll let you get back to it," Jillian said. "I'm sure he'll hassle you again at some point. Don't be afraid to stick up for yourself, although you should probably be a little more polite than I was just now. Have a good night."

She walked away before Kelly could say anything. She wanted to call after Jillian to wait, to just talk to her like she used to, but she didn't want Jillian to shut down again. Maybe she just needed more time. Well, if Kelly had anything, she had persistence, and she had patience. If Jillian thought she could continue waiting Kelly out, she didn't know what she was in for.

CHAPTER EIGHT

Jillian was hiding from Kelly. No matter how much she tried to spin it or justify it to herself, the facts were clear: she was hiding. She knew it was the height of cowardice to hunker down in her office on Friday, but she simply couldn't face Kelly so soon after what had happened in her office the night before. Ezra was bewildered but followed her directions. She thought she detected a note of reproach in his voice when he reported how disappointed Kelly was, but she ignored it and hung up on him. Thankfully, he didn't seem to have any idea of what had gone on between her and Kelly, and she wanted to keep it that way.

She desperately needed the weekend to try to reset her brain. She drove up to the lake early on Saturday, but it didn't do her any good; she kept remembering telling Kelly about Jerome and wondering what Kelly would think of the cabin. When she got home on Sunday evening, she even considered going back on the FindHer app. She could meet someone her own age, someone she didn't work with, have some actually meaningless sex…

The idea should have appealed to her, but instead, it made her strangely guilty. She'd probably just end up fantasizing about Kelly again anyway, and that wasn't fair to anyone.

Thursday night had been a massive error in judgment on her part. The safest thing to do would have been to keep her distance, to leave Kelly to her actual job and her nice, age-appropriate boyfriend. But when she saw Kelly across the floor on Monday, she knew her plan of avoiding her entirely wasn't going to work. She missed her too much. It was impossible to completely ignore the last two weeks, how smart and funny and inconveniently likable Kelly was, and she was *right there*. The way she looked around when Jillian waved at her was ridiculously adorable, and she felt her heart do a painful little flip at the sight. She deepened her resolve to avoid actual conversation with Kelly unless it was about work. That seemed safe enough.

She stuck to that for all of twelve hours, most of which she spent in client meetings nowhere near Kelly and free from temptation. But when she heard Leon spouting off the usual belligerent nonsense he threw at his junior associates, she was across the floor and intervening before she even realized what she was doing. She'd seen firsthand what level of work Kelly was capable of, and she was damned if she was going to let Leon damage her confidence. She left right after that, not trusting herself to be alone with Kelly in a nearly empty office.

In the weeks that followed, Kelly seemed to be inadvertently doing her best to push Jillian to the limits of her self-control. They were tiny little things, and she knew she was being ridiculous, but it was eating at her all the same. The next time she decided to vent her spleen by going to the far side of the floor to annoy Leon, she noticed Kelly had added a little Funko Pop! of Bob the ignominiously named slasher to her desk. Whenever Kelly ordered dinner from the Italian restaurant where they'd eaten the night they'd kissed, she'd get an extra piece of focaccia and leave it on Ezra's desk to give to Jillian. She was growing out her bangs, and occasionally, she wore the narrow scarf from her first day as a headband to keep them out of her eyes. The sight of it instantly made Jillian want to shove her up against the nearest wall and mark her up all over again.

It was almost a given that she'd cave, and she only lasted three weeks. Self-denial had never been one of her strong suits, and with Kelly, she already knew what she was missing out on. Kelly asked her through Ezra for help on her newest pro bono case, and like a fool, Jillian agreed to stay late with her one Friday night. To their credit, they did get a lot done before they looked at each other at exactly the same moment and moved toward each other like magnets.

The instant Kelly's lips touched hers, Jillian knew she was done for. She half-heartedly tried to break off the kiss, but they could both tell her heart wasn't in it. She pulled Kelly's body flush against hers and basked in the softness of her lips, the smell of her perfume, the warmth of her hands as she held Jillian close.

"Wait a second," Jillian murmured, a brief flash of sanity hitting her. "Hold on, what about Dan?"

Kelly stared at her. "Dan? What about him?"

"I thought you got back together."

"What are you even talking about?" Kelly asked, sounding truly baffled.

"The day he was here, you said he wanted to get back together? I guess I assumed..." Now that she thought about it, Kelly had never actually said she was seeing Dan again.

Kelly laughed softly. "There you go, assuming again. No, I told him no because...well, actually, because of you."

Jillian froze. If Kelly was making major life decisions because of her, this had already gone way too far, and she needed to call it off before it started.

Before she could panic too much, Kelly said, "Not that

I thought we were going to…to *date* or anything, but I just knew that I couldn't go back to the way things were before after we, um, you know."

"Well, that clears some things up," Jillian said, relieved. "In that case, do you want to come over and 'um, you know' again?"

"Oh, shut up," Kelly said, blushing, but she couldn't hide her grin as she nodded.

Jillian hesitated, knowing that Kelly probably wouldn't want to hear what she had to say next. "Listen, I still think this is a bad idea, and it could go horribly wrong, so we'll have to keep it really, really quiet. And I'm not ready to date right now, I'm just not. So if that's a deal-breaker for you…"

"It's not," Kelly said quickly. "I get it. I'm fine with it being just, friends with benefits or whatever you want to call it."

Jillian studied her. Kelly certainly sounded earnest enough, and nothing in her face gave any indication she wasn't being honest. It made sense, really. Surely at some point, she would grow tired of sleeping with a prickly, work-obsessed commitment-phobe twenty years her senior and want an actual relationship with someone else, and when that happened, Jillian would be the first to cheer her on. Until then, she might as well wring every bit of enjoyment she could out of the situation.

❖

"Oh, oh, oh, oh, oh, right there, don't stop!" Kelly's voice rose to a shriek as she braced herself on the headboard and ground her hips against Jillian's face while she came. After she finished, she collapsed on the bed next to Jillian. "I really liked the idea of sitting on your face, but it was kind of more of a workout than I expected," she said, breathing heavily.

Jillian snickered. "Come on, you've got youthful vigor on your side. Where's your stamina?"

"Hey, I'm too busy working a hundred hours a week to go to the gym right now," Kelly said, rolling her eyes.

Jillian laughed affectionately and kissed her. "Some of that's your own fault, you know. If you weren't such a good person, you wouldn't be spending so much time on pro bono work."

"Yeah, I know, but it makes me feel better about things like helping Leon and Greg get Bernie Madoff Lite off on a technicality," Kelly said ruefully.

"That needs to be the last time Leon's name is ever mentioned in this bed," Jillian said with a shudder.

Kelly raised her eyebrows. "What, hate-sex role-play doesn't do it for you?"

Jillian pretended to retch. "Get the hell out of my house," she ordered, and they both dissolved into laughter. Once she'd regained her composure, she said, "But seriously, is there anything in that arena you'd like to try? Anything from before that you liked or didn't like?"

"Actually, yeah," Kelly said a little nervously. "I was wondering if you could maybe be a little more..."

Jillian waited in trepidation, wondering what she was too embarrassed to say. Kelly had seemed to enjoy everything they'd done last time, but maybe now she was working up the nerve to admit she wasn't really into Jillian taking control the way she had.

Finally, Kelly seemed to steel herself. "I was wondering if you could maybe be a little *meaner* to me," she said, her cheeks turning pink and her eyes avoiding Jillian's.

"Kelly Lattimore! At this point, I should really know better than to think I know what you're going to say." This was better than she could have dared hope for.

"Not every time," Kelly said, looking embarrassed but determined. "I think you could tell I like it when you compliment me. But sometimes, maybe you might need to, you know, teach me a lesson or just throw me down and have your way with me."

Jillian was rendered speechless for a moment. This was a point against the existence of karma because she'd never done anything good enough in her life to deserve this. All sorts of possibilities flashed across her mind, each more erotic than the last.

"Is…is that okay with you? I don't *need* it or anything. I've never actually done it before, but I liked what we did last time, and I've been, um, thinking about it a lot," Kelly said, watching her anxiously.

"It's more than okay with me," Jillian assured her. "Very, very much more than okay."

"Oh good," Kelly said, relief spreading across her face.

Jillian ran her hand down Kelly's back and grabbed her ass hard as Kelly moaned. "Why don't you tell me some of the things you've been thinking about?" she whispered.

Kelly bit her lip. "You could…you could pull my hair."

Jillian threaded her fingers through Kelly's hair and tugged gently. "Like that?"

"Harder," Kelly panted.

Jillian obliged, and Kelly ground their hips together, gasping with pleasure. Soon, they were making out again, tongues darting in and out of each other's mouths as their bodies moved together. Jillian rolled on top and raised up on her forearms, looking down at Kelly. "Can I tie you up?" she whispered.

Kelly swallowed hard and nodded, so Jillian went to her trusty nightstand drawer. She had to dig to find what she was looking for but finally she emerged with a pair of long burgundy silk sashes.

"What, you don't have any handcuffs in there?" Kelly asked. She sounded relieved, and Jillian knew she'd made the right choice.

"Oh, I do," Jillian said with a leer. "Ropes too. But I thought it might be good to start off slowly, ease into things since it's totally new to you."

Kelly lay back and looked at her. "How do you want me?"

The sight of Kelly lying there, so eager and trusting and willing to take whatever Jillian would give her, was doing things to her body she hadn't felt in a long time. "Every single way I can think of," she practically growled.

Kelly's eyelids fluttered with lust, but she said, "Okay, but that's not actually helpful right now," and gave Jillian a knowing smirk.

"Oh, so that's how it's going to be?" Jillian said, straddling Kelly and pinning her to the bed as she gasped. "You're trying out the bratty sub thing, huh?"

Kelly moaned and thrust her hips against Jillian's. "I guess you'd better—oh, fuck—better punish me."

Jillian climbed off, and Kelly whimpered in dismay at the loss of friction. "Get on all fours," she ordered, and Kelly hurried to obey. Jillian tied first one hand and then the other to the headboard with the sashes, making sure they were secure but not uncomfortably tight.

"I assume you know what a safe word is?" she asked. Kelly nodded, and Jillian slapped her ass gently. "Answer me when I talk to you," she snapped.

"Yes, I know what a safe word is," Kelly said meekly.

"Pick one," Jillian said.

Kelly thought for a second. "Objection?" she suggested.

Jillian couldn't help laughing. "Objection it is," she agreed. "I can't believe I never thought of using that before."

The mood turned serious again, and the only sounds filling the room were sharp smacks and Kelly's moans as Jillian spanked her until her ass was bright red and she was biting the pillow to muffle her cries. Jillian only stopped when her hand started getting too sore to continue the barrage. She considered switching to a paddle or a riding crop, but she was still cautious of overwhelming Kelly with too much at once.

Instead, she put on the same strap-on as last time and fucked Kelly from behind, renewing the markings on her ass whenever they started to fade. The view was glorious, the dark silk sashes beautifully contrasting with her milky skin, the long, smooth curve of her back leading to the bright red of her ass, the strap-on sliding in and out effortlessly as Kelly cried out incoherently. Jillian hardly ever came while wearing the strap-on, but this time, she came within minutes, then shook it off and kept going.

Kelly's moans were getting louder and closer together, and Jillian thought she was probably on the brink. She reached a hand around Kelly's body to rub at her clit, and a moment later, Kelly was shrieking her name. Jillian could feel a slight tug on the strap-on as Kelly's body clutched at it through her orgasm. To her utter shock, she found herself coming again, riding it out before collapsing on top of Kelly, who had sprawled out on the bed beneath her.

"Oof," Kelly said, laughing softly.

"I guess you might like to be able to breathe at some point," Jillian said, clambering off her and starting to untie her hands.

"Breathing is good, yeah," Kelly said, rolling onto her side and smiling.

Jillian tossed the sashes aside and held Kelly in her arms. "How are you feeling?" she asked.

"Amazing," Kelly said dreamily. "A little sore, but otherwise, unbelievably good. Kind of like I'm floating."

"Sit tight, I'll be right back," Jillian said. She went to the kitchen to get a bottle of Gatorade, then detoured to the bathroom and grabbed some cocoa butter lotion before rejoining Kelly in bed. She had Kelly roll onto her stomach again and gently rubbed the lotion onto her ass, which had faded to barely a darker pink than its normal shade.

She spooned Kelly for a while as they shared the Gatorade, passing the bottle back and forth and trying not to spill the bright blue liquid onto the sheets. She felt worn out from both the spanking and topping, and she thought she probably needed the electrolytes as much as Kelly did.

"Still feeling okay?" she asked.

"Mm-hmm," Kelly said drowsily. "Tired."

Jillian knew she should send Kelly home. Letting her stay overnight might blur the lines of what they were doing, risked getting into dangerous territory. She could already feel herself starting to panic a little at the thought. But Kelly was warm in her arms, and Jillian could feel her slow, steady breathing and didn't have the heart to wake her. How much harm could one night possibly do anyway, she thought as she dropped off to sleep.

CHAPTER NINE

Kelly's mouth felt sticky and gross when she awoke. She realized she'd fallen asleep embarrassingly quickly last night, not even taking the time to brush her teeth. Jillian was still sound asleep next to her, her arm slung loosely across Kelly's waist. Kelly hesitated, not wanting to wake her, but eventually, her bladder made the decision for her. She slipped out of bed as gently as she could and tiptoed to the bathroom. After she brushed her teeth with her finger, she went back to the bedroom. Jillian had sprawled out in her absence. The morning sun peeking in through the blinds sent soft rays of light across her sleeping face. Kelly smiled at the sight. Jillian was usually so good at keeping her expression tightly controlled that it felt like Kelly was getting away with something seeing her so relaxed in sleep.

Her clothes were scattered across the floor where Jillian had thrown them the night before, but eventually, she tracked them all down and pulled them on. Remembering how quickly Jillian had ushered her out the door the first time, she figured she probably wouldn't want Kelly to stick around now, either. She was surprised Jillian had let her stay overnight, and she really didn't want to overstay her welcome any more than she already had. She turned to look at Jillian's peaceful form one more time, then left as quietly as she could.

They settled into a routine after that. Jillian continued to be paranoid about anyone at the firm finding out, so they staggered their departure times in the evening and their arrival times if Kelly stayed over. She tried not to too often, but whenever Jillian dominated her, she felt so hazy and comfortable afterward that it was almost inevitable that she'd fall asleep.

To be honest, she preferred staying at Jillian's; it was far nicer than her own apartment, closer to the office, and had no roommates to worry about. Sometimes on weekends, she'd bring her laptop with her, and they'd sit side by side on the couch, working in companionable silence or bouncing ideas off each other in between bouts of scorchingly hot sex. They never went out in public anywhere for fear of running into someone from work, but they'd order in sometimes. Sitting there at Jillian's kitchen table, trading take-out containers, Kelly had to remind herself that they weren't dating, that that wasn't something either of them even wanted.

She knew at least some of Jillian's paranoia was well-founded. Leon was petty enough, and his mutual animosity with Jillian strong enough, that it was entirely plausible he'd make trouble for Kelly just to get at Jillian if he knew. At the same time, all the sneaking around and pretending not to be overly interested in each other at work was starting to get to her. It reminded her uncomfortably of her parents' illicit relationship. She hesitantly mentioned this to Jillian, not wanting to upset the delicate equilibrium they'd found but also growing tired of being treated like a shameful secret.

"I can see how you might feel that way, yeah," Jillian said thoughtfully after Kelly had finally worked up the nerve to broach the subject.

She'd strategically waited until shortly after they'd done a scene, her slight anxiety about the upcoming conversation keeping her from dropping off to sleep like usual. She'd been very, very good, and she knew Jillian was especially pleased with her and, therefore, perhaps predisposed to be more lenient than usual about secrecy. Jillian was still holding her close, rubbing aloe onto the welts she'd left along her ass and the backs of her thighs.

After she finished, she kissed Kelly's shoulder tenderly and said, "Tell you what. Why don't we spend the weekend at my cabin? It's the offseason, so it's really unlikely anyone who knows you will be around. Admittedly, there are only two restaurants in town, and they're both terrible, but we could at least go out in public together."

It stung a little that Jillian's first thought was still secrecy, but it *did* sound nice, and Kelly recognized that it probably took a lot for her to even offer it, so she agreed. Miraculously, they were both finished by 7:00 that Friday, so they made the two-hour drive north that night instead of waiting until Saturday.

Jillian had described the cabin to her in the car, but it was still a surprise just how different it was from her trendy and modern city apartment. Even Jillian's luxury car looked out of place parked next to the tiny wooden structure. Kelly fell in love with it even before Jillian had finished turning on the lights. It smelled of pine and the old smoke of countless fires in the stone fireplace. There was a little screened-in porch off the living room with a pair of wicker rocking chairs facing out toward the lake, which was currently shrouded in darkness. While Jillian got a fire going, Kelly stood on the dark porch listening to the hum of insects outside. Suddenly, a haunting cry tore through the relative quiet, and she started a little.

"It's a loon," Jillian said, coming out to join her from the living room. "They'll be migrating south in a week or two. I'm glad we got up here before then so you could hear them."

The loon let out a series of trills even louder than its first wail. Another one called back from farther away. It was cold out on the porch, and Kelly shivered a little. Jillian put an arm around her to warm her as they listened to the loons' chorus for a few minutes until the birds seemed to decide they were done.

"Come on, let's go sit by the fire," Jillian said, leading Kelly inside.

Kelly looked around the little living room while Jillian went to the kitchenette to make them peppermint tea. What looked like a homemade bookshelf held a collection of worn paperbacks, nature guides, a couple of outdated state statute and case books, and a random assortment of jigsaw puzzles and board games. The walls were bare except for a framed map of the lake above the birchwood mantel. She pulled one of the state statutes off the shelf and flipped through it, stopping at a page marked up with notes. Most were in what she recognized as Jillian's handwriting, the rest in a scrawling script that must have been Jerome's.

Jillian returned and handed her a steaming mug. "The librarians gave us those when they got the new editions in. The relevant property laws hadn't changed, so they were still useful to us," she explained.

"You really put the work in to help him, didn't you? No wonder he left you this place," Kelly said.

Jillian shrugged. "He knew I'd keep it instead of selling it to be turned into condos or a giant McMansion. There's a lot of history in these walls. I can't wait for you to see the lake tomorrow."

They sat on the couch drinking their tea, watching the fire crackle and snap while Jillian regaled her with stories of canoeing, swimming, and fishing during her childhood.

It was hard to imagine Jillian in waders putting worms on a fishhook, but she swore it was true. "I think there are pictures somewhere," she said.

"Do your parents still live here?" Kelly asked. She didn't know why the question hadn't occurred to her earlier.

"No, they moved to Florida after they retired," Jillian said. "We're not terribly close. They've never been super happy about the gay thing, and even beyond that, we never had much in common. We talk maybe once a month, mostly about the weather."

She didn't seem unhappy about it, but Kelly thought it sounded like a lonely life. At least she had her mom. Even if she couldn't confide every detail to her, she still knew beyond a doubt that her mom loved her and enjoyed her company.

They moved into the bedroom soon after that, which was barely big enough to hold a double bed and a small wardrobe. They had slow, quiet sex, a far cry from their usual activities, but it felt right for the setting. When Jillian switched off the lights after they'd gotten ready for bed, the room was so pitch-black, Kelly couldn't see her hand when she waved it in front of her face. The bedroom was cold, but she burrowed into the down comforter and pressed her body against Jillian's, and soon, she was asleep.

She woke up early but felt totally refreshed after one of the soundest nights of sleep of her life. She could hear Jillian out in the main part of the cabin and went out to join her. She was standing over the little two-burner propane stove making scrambled eggs and bacon while the coffee maker hissed and sputtered on the counter.

"Good morning," Kelly said brightly, kissing her cheek.

Jillian yawned and replied, "You're awfully chipper this morning. Sleep well?"

"The best," Kelly said, and Jillian smiled.

"I always sleep well up here too. I think it's the fresh mountain air and the total darkness. Mugs and plates are up there, and utensils are in that drawer," Jillian told her, and they finished making breakfast together.

They brought their food out to the little table out on the porch, even though it was still chilly out there. The lake was in full view now, and it lived up to Jillian's billing. Kelly could see why developers had been salivating to get their hands on this spot and also why Jerome had been so reluctant to sell. Most of the trees along the shoreline were pine, but occasional pops of New England fall color dotted the view. The water stretched out clear and blue, occasional little islands interrupting the flow. Gentle mountains rose in the distance as far as the eye could see.

"Wow," Kelly said softly, awestruck. She realized Jillian was watching her instead of the lake and smiling.

"That's the correct response," Jillian said. "Anyone who doesn't love this view isn't someone worth knowing. The first time I brought my ex-wife up here, she asked if I'd looked into getting satellite TV installed. That should have been my warning sign."

"Who needs TV when you have *this*?" Kelly asked incredulously, gesturing out at the lake. She ignored the reference to Jillian's ex-wife, about whom she was desperately curious but reluctant to ask.

Jillian nodded vigorously. "Exactly! I do have high-speed internet—well, as high-speed as you can get up here—but only so I can work if I need to. Otherwise, it's a tech-free zone. I get enough of that back in the city. Do you want to go for a canoe ride after breakfast?"

Kelly agreed, and after leisurely finishing their breakfast, they headed onto the water. They passed two other canoes, a kayak, and a little motorboat puttering along, but otherwise, they seemed like the only ones on the lake. Jillian sat in the stern and steered, correcting Kelly's posture and grip on the paddle. She'd done a little canoeing at summer camp, but that had been years ago, and she was rusty. Eventually, they made it to their destination, one of the islands visible from Jillian's porch, and tied the canoe up to one of the docks.

"What is this place?" Kelly asked curiously.

"It's a church," Jillian said simply and led the way to a path.

Kelly followed, a little baffled. It definitely didn't look like a church. There weren't any buildings at all on the tiny island that she could see. The path wound through a patch of woods and opened into a clearing, and then she understood. Rows of pews were laid out right under the trees facing a stone altar and a sweeping view of the lake.

"This is so cool," Kelly said, looking around.

Jillian pointed at a small shed Kelly hadn't noticed. "There's a pump organ in there, and that's also where they store all the hymnals. They only have services in the summer, but people can come visit on their own whenever."

"So it's an actual functioning church?" Kelly said, peeking in through the shed window. She could see huge stacks of books inside.

"Oh yeah," Jillian said. "My parents got married here. So did my best friend from law school. She's actually a partner at our firm, but you probably don't know her since she's in the real estate division. Her name's Serena Ma."

The name was familiar, but Kelly didn't think she'd ever actually met Serena, so she shook her head.

"Well, anyway, I introduced her to it. And to her husband, too, for that matter. I'm still proud of that one," Jillian said smugly.

"Where'd you get married?" Kelly asked as they walked back to the canoe.

Jillian grimaced. "This big fancy hotel ballroom downtown. It was nice enough, but it could have been anywhere, you know? There was nothing unique about it. Tessa had her heart set on a big black-tie thing, though. Weddings are weird. You spend a small fortune on one night, and then ten years later, you find yourself screaming at each other over who's going to get some five-dollar souvenir from a trip you don't even remember, and you start to wonder what it was all for anyway."

Kelly hesitated, but her curiosity overcome her nerves. "What exactly happened between you, if you don't mind me asking?"

Jillian inhaled audibly, but she looked contemplative rather than angry or offended. "I've asked myself that question plenty of times. It feels like a cliché to say we grew apart. And that's not quite right, anyway. We're both pretty driven, which drew us together at first. She's a ballerina—well, retired now—and you can imagine how much dedication and long hours she had to put into getting to that level. When she retired from dancing, she expected me to take a step back from work too, but I don't think she ever understood that my career is as important to me as hers was to her. Cue the fighting, the drama, etc. until she finally left. I'm glad that part of my life's over. It was painful, but I learned my lesson. I'm definitely never getting married again."

"I can see how that would make you jaded," Kelly said. "I can't say I have the most romantic view of marriage, either, not with my parents."

"I can't believe watching dear old Benton mess up two women's lives didn't make you want to run right out and get hitched. Or four, counting you and Sarah," Jillian said.

Kelly shrugged. "I guess Sarah's not too jaded if she's marrying that Ted guy."

"I wonder if she'll invite you to the wedding," Jillian said wryly.

"Oh, didn't I tell you? She asked me to be her maid of honor," Kelly deadpanned, and Jillian laughed.

They had lunch in one of the two local restaurants and dinner in the other. Jillian was right that they were terrible, but Kelly appreciated being out in public instead of feeling like they always had to hide. All in all, she thought it was a successful weekend.

❖

When she got home on Sunday, she FaceTimed her mom for their usual weekly check-in. "How's your weekend been? Did you get a chance to do anything besides work?" her mom asked.

Kelly hesitated. She hadn't told her about what had been going on with Jillian, which more or less limited her conversational topics to work. But she thought about Jillian talking to her parents about the weather once a month and decided to confide in her mom.

"Wow," her mom said when she finished, eyebrows sky-high. "Are you *sure* she's not married? Because your dad told me he was divorced when we met, and by the time I found out the truth, I was already pregnant with you."

"Yes, I'm sure," Kelly said patiently. "She's at the office almost as much as I am. She doesn't have time for a wife *and* a mistress. How did you deal with all the secrecy and having so little time together and stuff?"

Her mom frowned in concentration. "I never really minded it, to be honest. I didn't want to be tied down by a full-time relationship, so it seemed like the perfect situation for me. I regret how it affected you, though. In retrospect, I would do a lot of things differently. But not all of it because it gave me my awesome, smart, amazing daughter."

"Ugh, Mom," Kelly said, rolling her eyes. "Could you be any cheesier?"

Her mom laughed, then said, "But seriously, I just want to know that you're happy and being treated well. You should be with someone who's proud to be with you. If having to sneak around bothers you this much, it might not be the right relationship for you."

"It's not a relationship," Kelly insisted.

"Sure," her mom said skeptically. "Have you told your grandparents about her? I'm a little worried about how they'd react."

"God, no, and I don't plan to."

"That's probably for the best. You're already on thin ice with them because of Sarah running into you at work."

"Which is weird because they know where I work. Why didn't they tell her or Ted I might be there?" She didn't know why the thought hadn't occurred to her earlier.

"Typical Lattimore mind games," her mom said scathingly. "Or more likely, just carelessness. They probably didn't even think about it. Have you talked to them recently?"

"Nope." She'd left her grandmother a voice mail a few weeks ago, but she hadn't actually spoken to either of her grandparents since before she'd started her job. They were probably too busy with Sarah's impending nuptials. She tried and failed not to feel bitter about the thought.

"That's their loss. Anyway, back to your Jillian situation. Maybe you should take some time to think about if this is really working for you."

After they hung up, her mom's words weighed on her

mind. She liked what she and Jillian were doing. She *really* liked it. But it would be nice if she could do something as simple as stop by Jillian's office to say hi without her freaking out about it. It might be time to give some serious thought to what she really wanted.

CHAPTER TEN

The sex was just as good as before, but Kelly was a little withdrawn in the days following their weekend away. Jillian didn't understand it. Hadn't it been exactly what Kelly had said she wanted, a chance to go out without worry for a change? Maybe she was growing weary of their arrangement and was trying to figure out how to end it.

An anxious tightening filled her chest at the thought. She'd gotten used to things as they were, and it wasn't easy to find someone she was this compatible with in bed. Several times, she was on the brink of broaching the subject herself, perhaps even ripping off the Band-Aid and calling it off before Kelly could.

One night when Kelly came over, she dodged Jillian's kiss and sat at the kitchen table instead. She set her palms down determinedly and took a deep breath, and Jillian's heart started going about a thousand beats a minute.

"Look," Kelly said at last. "I understand how important keeping this quiet is to you, but if you can't loosen up even a tiny bit, then I…I can't do this anymore."

Jillian stared at her. "What? I *did* loosen up. What about the cabin?"

"And that was a great trip, but you literally picked it because no one would be there. I really don't think I'm asking for a lot. I'm not saying we need to go around the office telling everyone. I just want to be able to say hi to you in the hallway or eat dinner together if we're working late. Things we were doing *before* we started sleeping together, by the way," Kelly said in a single breath.

"Wow. Um, okay. Just give me a minute to process here," Jillian said. She didn't know if this was better or worse than what she'd been expecting. Her mind whirled. Maybe Kelly had a point, and she was being overly cautious. The best-case scenario was that she'd lighten up, and they could continue on as they had been with nobody the wiser. She'd never been one to rely on things working out for the best, though. Next, she imagined the news spreading all over the firm, all the little jibes she'd have to endure from Leon, the judgmental looks from people like Tom Sullivan, even possible liability for the firm…

"Are you okay?" Kelly asked.

"I'm fine," Jillian insisted, pressing a hand to her chest and willing her heart to slow down.

"You don't look fine," Kelly said, watching her with concern.

Jillian sighed deeply. "Okay, I'm not fine. I'm freaking the fuck out. I just keep thinking about everyone knowing, and what if I get the firm sued, and everything I've been doing for the last twenty years goes up in smoke and—"

"Jillian, breathe," Kelly said, gripping her hands across the table. "I'm not going to tell anyone or sue the firm. I actually…I actually had an idea about that."

Kelly's touch was grounding, and to her enormous relief, Jillian found her breathing and heart rate returning to normal. "I'm feeling better now. What's your idea?"

"I kind of, um, looked it up in the employee handbook?" Kelly said, her voice trailing up at the end.

Jillian stared at her. "Is that a question?"

Kelly flushed a little. "No. I looked it up in the employee handbook," she said more firmly. "It says that partners and associates can have, quote, 'personal relationships of a romantic and/or sexual nature,' as long as the partner doesn't have any supervisory authority over the associate's work in any way. And you have to register it with HR."

"Well, I'm really glad the employee handbook allows us to be fuck buddies," Jillian said. Kelly gave her a reproachful look. She knew it was crass, but there was no point in tiptoeing around it.

"Doesn't this solve at least one of your problems, though?" Kelly asked. "It'd take care of the liability issue. You're not my supervisor anymore, and you don't have authority over Leon, much as I know you'd like to."

Jillian couldn't help smiling at that, but she forced herself to stay on topic. "Can you seriously imagine marching into the HR office and telling little seventy-year-old, almost-became-a-nun Carol that we want to register that we're sleeping together? And as confidential as those things are supposed to be, you can't tell me no one would find out about it."

Kelly bit her lip, which didn't help Jillian's concentration. "Would that really be the worst thing in the world? I mean, look at that guy over in tax, what's-his-name, the partner who's dating Madison Shafer? As long as we keep acting professional at work…"

"Oh, come on, think about it. Really think about it, Kelly. It's all well and good for Alex fucking Donahue to date an associate, but it's totally different for me. The MILF and cougar jokes are already writing themselves. And it's not like Madison is coming out of it totally clean, either. You wait and see, if they stay together, I bet she'll move to another firm within a year because no one will think she earned the job here based on her own merit," Jillian said.

"She was fifth in her class at Columbia Law School," Kelly said, outraged. "And she was already working here when they started dating."

Jillian snorted and shook her head. "You think that matters? The stories I could tell you, honestly. The *only* saving grace I can see about us would be that you're not a guy. A female partner dating a male junior associate would lose any credibility whatsoever. This situation is about the only time I can see being a lesbian working in my favor. And I know you don't care about staying here long-term, but I do."

"Well, if that's how you feel, then that's how you feel," Kelly said sadly. "But honestly? I feel like you're pulling a Benton, and I'm not going to stick around like my mom did for a decade and be treated like your dirty little secret when we're not even doing anything wrong. Let me know if you ever change your mind." She got up and headed for the door.

"Wait, you're leaving right now?" Jillian asked incredulously. "What about one last roll in the hay for old time's sake?"

Kelly gave her a look that could only be described as pitying. "See you around, Jillian," she said as she left.

Jillian sat and stared at the closed door of her apartment for a long time.

❖

Jillian tried valiantly not to care, but it was hard to move on when the office, her apartment, and now the cabin were all tainted by Kelly's presence. The worst of it was that even now that she could ostensibly act friendlier to Kelly, seeing her just made Jillian feel bad, so she was avoiding her as much as ever.

She found her attention slipping at work to the point where Chris Hendricks pulled her aside after a meeting and quietly asked if she was okay. While Chris was one of her favorite coworkers, he wasn't known for his emotional intelligence, so if *he* had picked up on her mood, she desperately needed to do something about the situation.

"JB! What a nice surprise," Serena Ma said when Jillian entered her office. "I feel like I haven't seen you in a million years. What's new?"

"I'm going to preface all this by saying I just put you on retainer for when I buy my own place again, so you're my lawyer now, and this conversation falls under attorney-client privilege," Jillian said.

Serena's eyes widened dramatically. "Uh-oh. Okay, noted. What happened? Did you push Tessa in front of a moving train? Because I don't feel qualified to help you with that."

"Thankfully, not quite that bad," Jillian said and filled her in. By the time she finished, Serena was staring at her, open-mouthed.

"This is so un-Jillian-like, I don't even know where to start," Serena said. "Well, not the casual rebound sex or the workaholism or the fear of commitment. That's all very on-brand for you."

"Thanks a lot," Jillian said sourly.

Serena held out a placating hand. "Sorry. You know I love you, JB. I'm just…wow. How are you feeling about it all?"

"I don't really know, honestly," Jillian said. "Relieved in a way because there's no more worry about people finding out. I guess she could still tell people, but she said she wouldn't, and I believe her. But also…it was really good sex."

"It'd have to be to get you to take this level of risk," Serena said with a snicker.

Jillian nodded. "I miss that part of it. And we had fun hanging out, too. We went to the cabin a couple weeks ago."

"Whoa, hold up," Serena said. "You took your friend with benefits to your super-special cabin, your favorite place on the planet? You didn't even take *me* there until we'd known each other for over a year. Now I'm really curious about this girl."

"I was trying to keep her happy so she'd keep sleeping with me," Jillian said, shifting in her seat uncomfortably.

"Uh-huh," Serena said skeptically. "And yet, you let that crash and burn anyway, all because you're afraid to say hi to her in the hallway and sign a piece of paper for HR?"

Jillian felt her hackles rising. "Wait a minute, whose side are you on? Can you imagine what would happen if people found out?"

Serena sighed and said, "Of course I'm on your side, I'm just trying to help you get some perspective here. I won't deny that it could be rough going, at least at first, and you might have to prove yourself all over again to some people. But most of your clients won't care about you dating an associate as long as you keep getting results, if they even hear about it at all. It's not like you'd be working on cases together anymore. As for around the office, eventually, there'll be some new hot gossip, and people will lose interest. You'd just have to ride it out. You got through everyone gossiping about your divorce, right?"

"Everyone gossiped about my divorce?" Jillian asked.

"Of course not," Serena said hurriedly.

Jillian ignored that for now, although she'd corner her about it later once Serena had thought she'd forgotten about it. "Besides, it's not just me I have to worry about. Kelly's so smart, and she's doing really well here. I hate to think of people not taking her seriously because of me. Not to mention that prick Leon gives her a tough enough time just by being himself. She's already almost as good a lawyer as he is and a million times better as a person, not to mention infinitely better looking."

"I'm glad you've found such a great *friend* now that you're single," Serena said with an air of unimpeachable innocence. "It sounds like you've warned her of the risks, and she's okay with them, and she's not even planning to stay in Big Law anyway."

Jillian glared at her suspiciously, but Serena was a tough nut for even her to crack, and her face gave away nothing. Serena was one of the smartest people she'd ever met and also one of the few who really, truly knew her. Both Serena and Kelly had accused her of acting out of fear. One of them she could discount easily enough, but both? By the time she rose to return to her own office, she'd made her decision.

Instead of turning to the right when she got off the elevator, she went left instead. Steeling herself, she marched to Kelly's office. Kelly was engrossed in something on her computer, giving Jillian the opportunity to watch her as she approached. She was frowning in concentration at the screen, but her eyes lit up, and she let out a little "aha" of victory under her breath as she found what she was looking for. Jillian had to cover her mouth for a second to hide her smile.

Kelly didn't notice Jillian until she was standing right in front of her desk, and she finally looked up. "Um, hi," she said.

"Hi," Jillian said. "Are you working late tonight?"

"Define late. I feel like I live here," Kelly said ruefully. "Leon's got me working on three different cases at once, I have my own pro bono case, and Serena Ma just asked Leon if she could borrow me for something. Doesn't real estate have their own associates? She's your friend, right? Do you know what that's about?"

Jillian made a silent vow to murder Serena at the earliest opportunity. "No idea. I ask because I'll be here for a while, and I'm ordering Indian tonight. Do you want anything?"

Kelly just stared at her.

"It doesn't have to be Indian," Jillian said hurriedly. "You can pick. I just thought, you're working late, and I'm working late, and it might be nice to take a dinner break at the same time—"

"Indian's good," Kelly said, cutting her off. "That sounds...really good. Thanks."

"Cool," Jillian said, feeling anything but in the moment.

"Cool," Kelly agreed, a grin slowly spreading across her face.

"Anyway, Ezra will message you when he's getting the order together. See you later," Jillian said and beat a hasty retreat.

They ate in her office with the door open. The conversation mostly stuck to their current cases, but Kelly mentioned an upcoming fundraising gala being hosted by several large charitable organizations. The firm was a generous corporate donor and had bought several tables for partners and a handful of associates lucky enough to be chosen.

"Charlie Redfern won a ticket because he had the most billed hours of all the first-year associates this quarter, and I got one because I had the most pro bono hours," she explained.

Jillian rolled her eyes fondly. "Of course you did."

"The thing is…" Kelly said, twisting her hands anxiously. "I don't want to go. Did you look at the list of all the charities? One is the Lattimore Foundation. I doubt most of my relatives will be there, but Sarah's their marketing manager. She'll definitely go. What do I do? Should I give the ticket away?"

Jillian winced in sympathy. "Yikes. Don't give the ticket away. That's a *huge* get for a junior associate. It's face time with all the senior partners, plus a bunch of big names from all over town, including some of the nonprofits you might want to work for once you leave here. It'll look really bad for Leon if you turn it down, too. You definitely don't want to draw that kind of negative attention to yourself."

Kelly groaned and said, "I was afraid you'd say something like that. It's going to be so awkward, though."

"You handled it so well last time, and at least this time, you know in advance that she'll be there," Jillian pointed out. "Besides, I've been to this thing before. There's hundreds of people, it's huge. At most, you'll have to talk to her for, like, two seconds."

"Are *you* going?" Kelly asked hopefully.

"I wasn't planning to this year. Scheduling conflict," Jillian said. She'd always gone with Tessa before. Having someone to laugh and joke and dance with had made the whole ridiculous spectacle bearable, even fun. As disastrous as their marriage had been at the end, the good times haunted her more.

"Bummer," Kelly said. "Maybe I'll see if Dan's going."

"You know, I could probably move things around. What the hell, I'll go," Jillian said.

The beam that overtook Kelly's face was almost enough to distract Jillian from her own idiocy.

CHAPTER ELEVEN

It always comes down to carbs, Kelly thought inanely as Jillian clicked the handcuffs closed on her wrists. She hadn't intended to come home with Jillian tonight, but apparently, all it took to get her back in bed was a piece of naan.

She was getting a lot more than that—Jillian had haltingly agreed that they could go to HR in the morning—but in her heart of hearts, Kelly knew she'd be here right now even if that hadn't happened. It was hard to care too much, not when she could feel Jillian's lubed fingers circling her rim, gently opening her up enough to slip in a plug. She tried to press herself against Jillian's fingers, impatient to get on with it, but the instant she moved, Jillian pulled her hand away. When Kelly whimpered pleadingly, Jillian swatted her ass hard with a riding crop.

"None of that," Jillian said sternly. "I'm going to take as much time as I want, and I don't want to hear any more whining out of you."

It took all her self-restraint, but Kelly managed to stay quiet as Jillian teased her, taking far longer than necessary before finally sliding the plug fully inside. Kelly couldn't help a small sigh of pleasure, but Jillian allowed it.

"That feels better, doesn't it?" Jillian crooned, draping her body over Kelly's back and threading her fingers through her hair.

"Yes," Kelly whispered. When asked a direct question, she was not only allowed but required to answer. Jillian rewarded her with a rough tug on her hair and a nip at her neck, and Kelly cried out.

"You know, I'm being very nice to you," Jillian mused. "What do you say when someone's nice to you?"

"Thank you," Kelly said quietly.

"That's my good sweet girl," Jillian said, and Kelly had to bite back another whimper. "I knew the brattiness was just a phase. The truth is, you're a needy little slut who just wants to please me, aren't you?"

This time, Kelly couldn't hold in her moan, and Jillian spanked her again with the crop. "Yes, I want to be your good girl."

Jillian ran her hand gently down her back. "I'm going to let you show me how good you can be. Would you like that?"

"Oh please," Kelly begged.

Jillian sat back on her heels and caressed her, then began mercilessly hitting her ass and thighs with the crop over and over again.

She held it in as long as she could, but eventually, Kelly couldn't resist crying out with each blow. Every time Jillian struck her, her muscles clenched instinctively around the plug in her ass, further heightening the sensation. She dropped her head onto the bed and let her mind go totally blank, focusing only on the exquisitely painful pleasure rushing through her body. Everything that overwhelmed or worried her the rest of the time faded away, and all that remained was the sharp smacking sound and the biting sting of the crop.

"Baby, you look amazing like this," Jillian said with a

moan. "Just lying there taking what I give you, your ass all red from me, but I bet you can take more, can't you?"

Jillian's words washed over her, and for a second, she was too blissed out to answer, but she finally remembered how to speak. "A little more," she whispered.

"You're so good for me," Jillian murmured, spanking her a few more times. "And since you were so good, I'm going to let you have a reward. Get on your side."

Kelly could barely contain herself, but she didn't gasp from the thrum of excitement Jillian's promise sent rushing through her. Her hands still cuffed to the headboard, she rolled onto her side like Jillian told her to. Jillian lay down beside her with her head at Kelly's feet. It took some maneuvering, but finally, she positioned herself right in front of Kelly's face, her knee resting on Kelly's shoulder. The mouthwatering scent of her arousal filled Kelly's senses, and she whimpered in anticipation. She knew she had to wait for Jillian to give her the green light, though.

"Go ahead," Jillian breathed, apparently not feeling too patient herself.

Kelly dove in eagerly, relishing every moan and cry she drew out of Jillian. It was a little hard not being able to use her hands, and her arms were starting to get sore from being in the same position for so long, but she did her best. Jillian certainly seemed to be enjoying herself; she was releasing a steady stream of gasps and curses under her breath as Kelly licked and sucked at her.

Suddenly, she felt Jillian's tongue on her clit, and her brain short-circuited. She gasped against Jillian's skin, then went back to eating her out as best she could while Jillian proceeded to feast on her. Kelly was already so worked up from the spanking and Jillian's praise that it felt like hardly any time at all before she was on the brink.

"Can I come?" she asked breathlessly.

Jillian pulled away long enough to whisper, "Of course you can, my beautiful, perfect girl," then dove back in.

Sparks shot through Kelly's body as she crested over the edge, mind-melting pleasure rushing through every cell of her body. She shrieked and clutched Jillian's head between her thighs, Jillian's tongue still working her over as the sensation went on and on.

When it finally subsided, she only needed to suck at Jillian's clit for a minute before she was coming against Kelly's mouth with a cry.

Jillian slumped on the bed, then sat up and wiped off her mouth and chin before freeing Kelly's hands. She rubbed her thumbs gently over the red marks on Kelly's wrists where the handcuffs had chafed as Kelly moved onto her stomach again and rolled her shoulders to get the blood flowing.

"Let me know if this hurts," Jillian said, grasping the base of the plug and starting to ease it out of Kelly's ass.

"Mmmph," Kelly said incoherently, folding her arms under her chin and letting her eyes fall closed.

Her body was so relaxed that Jillian met with no resistance, and soon, Kelly felt her get up off the bed. Her mind drifted aimlessly, utterly content. Jillian might have been gone for thirty minutes or thirty seconds, it was impossible to say. When she came back, she rubbed aloe on Kelly's sore ass, then wrapped her in her arms. Kelly melted into her touch as Jillian stroked her side and softly kissed her neck.

"I'm glad you came over," Jillian whispered into her ear.

"I'm glad you bought me Indian food," Kelly replied.

Jillian let out a surprised laugh. "You must *really* like Indian food."

"Yeah, but mostly I really like *you,*" Kelly mumbled, and promptly fell asleep.

❖

"Thanks for coming down, I know you're busy," Serena Ma said, smiling brightly. "Coffee?"

"No thanks," Kelly said, shifting uncomfortably. She didn't want to be rude, but the truth was, she barely had a moment to spare, and she sincerely hoped this meeting wouldn't take long.

"Have a seat," Serena said, gesturing at one of the chairs opposite her desk.

Kelly perched on the edge of the chair. "Uh, what case did you want to see me about?"

"How are you finding life at the firm?" Serena asked, utterly ignoring Kelly's obvious desire to leave.

"Oh, it's fine. A lot of pressure, but I knew that coming in," Kelly said with a shrug. What on earth was this about?

Serena nodded sagely. "You're very lucky you ended up with Jillian for your first two weeks rather than Leon. She's a real force of nature, isn't she?"

Ah, Jillian. So it wasn't work-related at all. "Yeah, she's great."

"And how are you getting along with her?" Serena asked. Her tone was bland, almost disinterested, but she hadn't become one of the most successful attorneys in her division by being easy to read. She had to know; there was no other explanation.

Kelly decided to take the bull by the horns. She didn't have time to delicately dance around the subject. "Is this a shovel talk? 'Hurt my friend, and I'll have you murdered,' that sort of thing?"

Serena studied her appraisingly, and Kelly managed not to squirm in her seat. "I've known Jillian a long time," she said at last. "Almost as long as you've been alive. She doesn't need protection from you. She needs to be protected from herself. She's afraid to let herself be happy. I called you down here to get a sense for myself of just how much danger she's in right now."

"And what's your verdict?" Kelly asked, tension filling her body.

"There are too many fucking legal metaphors," Serena said exasperatedly, and Kelly let out a surprised laugh. "But I suppose the jury's still out, if we're sticking with that one. For what it's worth, I like you quite a bit so far, which is more than I can say for certain other people. Cough, Tessa, cough, cough. You seem like a straight shooter. You know what, what the hell. You have my approval."

Kelly sighed in relief. She knew how much Jillian valued Serena's opinion. "So you'd give it a green light, then? Since you don't like legal metaphors?"

"Ugh," Serena said. "Don't make me regret this, but, yes. Which probably means Jillian's going to freak out and mess it up at some point, I'm warning you now."

"She's already had her freak-out. I think you talked her down from it."

"That's assuming there'll only be one. I knew Tessa was wrong for her when she didn't balk at the wedding," Serena said skeptically. "Anyway, you'd better get back upstairs before Leon blows a gasket. I play a little game with myself where I see how many consecutive days I can avoid seeing him. My record is sixty-eight. I'm on a fifty-two day streak now, so I don't want him to come looking for you."

"Good luck," Kelly said with a laugh. She envied Serena's relatively Leon-free life.

She considered what Serena had said as she returned to her office. She was Jillian's best friend, but Kelly thought she was wrong this time. Jillian had gotten over her fear enough for them to go to HR together. There wasn't as much for her to freak out about now that they'd successfully crossed their biggest hurdle.

❖

"How about this one?" Kelly asked hopefully, holding up the dress she'd worn to her last spring formal in law school.

"Not fancy enough. This is a really swanky party, right? I think you need to buy something new," Allison said, shaking her head.

Kelly groaned. "I was afraid you'd say that. I don't have time to go shopping, and I'd really rather not spend the money, either."

"I know," Allison said sympathetically. "But think about how much better you'll feel about seeing Sarah if you go in knowing you look amazing. Not to mention the look on Jillian's face when she sees her hot-ass date."

"Oh my God, stop. We're not going *together*, we're just both going, and we're carpooling so I don't have to spend money on an Uber," Kelly insisted.

Allison smirked. "Sure, keep telling yourself that. And you totally didn't mention Dan to make her jealous, and *she* totally didn't decide to go because she was, in fact, jealous about you mentioning Dan."

"You're the worst. Why are we friends again?" Kelly said. Allison knew her far too well, and had instantly guessed at her motives when she'd recounted her conversation with Jillian about the gala.

"Shush, you know you love me. Hey, you should find out what dress Jillian's going to wear so you know what color corsage to get her," Allison said gleefully.

Kelly glared at her, but the effect was undercut by the snicker she couldn't hold in, and soon, they were both laughing.

It was a relief to finally be able to talk to Allison openly about her non-relationship with Jillian. They were still keeping it as quiet as possible, but they'd signed the required forms for a very surprised Carol in HR.

Kelly hadn't told anyone aside from her mom and Allison, and as far as she knew, Jillian had only told Serena. Jillian had eased up on her restrictions about their interactions in the office. It was nice to be able to have lunch together occasionally or chat if they happened to be in the elevator at the same time. Carol had assured them that the forms would stay confidential, but she couldn't do anything about any rumors that might start. So far, the news hadn't spread throughout the firm, but Jillian resignedly predicted it would only be a matter of time.

Although not for corsage purposes, Kelly did follow Allison's suggestion of asking Jillian what she was planning to wear to the gala the next time she was at her apartment.

"You can't really go too formal for this," Jillian said. "I mean, it's not the Met Gala, but think Oscar night, red-carpet type of dresses, preferably designer." She pulled some dresses from previous years out of her closet, and Kelly's heart sank. She didn't own anything close to nice enough, and buying something similar would cost a fortune.

"I don't even know where to buy something like that," Kelly said with a groan. "Let alone how I'll afford it. I already threw most of my last paycheck at my loans."

Jillian scrutinized the dresses on her bed, then selected a sparkly silver one. "Try this," she said, thrusting it into Kelly's arms.

Kelly slipped it on, but the zipper wouldn't go all the way up. It was a shame because the dress was beautiful, but she was afraid of ripping it.

"Oh yeah, that was the year Tessa moved out for a few months, and I kept forgetting to eat," Jillian mused. "I should probably give that one away. I'm sure it doesn't fit me anymore, either. How about this one?"

Kelly tried on half a dozen more of Jillian's dresses, but none of them were quite right. Jillian had bigger boobs and narrower shoulders than her, so some of them were tight where they shouldn't have been and baggy in all the wrong places. Jillian suggested having one altered, but Kelly didn't like the idea of her not being able to wear her own dress anymore.

"I'm not likely to wear most of these again," Jillian said with a shrug. "I only keep them around to wear to fancy weddings. I can stand to lose one. Wait a second, I have an idea."

She rummaged around in the back of the closet and finally emerged with a floor-length, seafoam green dress. Kelly pulled it on, and mercifully, it actually fit. It was simpler than the others, but the soft chiffon almost floated when she moved in it, and the color perfectly complemented the hazel of her eyes. She did a delighted little twirl in front of the mirror.

Jillian was watching her with a hungry look. "Fuck, it's hot to see you in my clothes. You should wear them more often. But also, take it off. Right now." Kelly hurried to obey, and Jillian followed suit.

Numerous orgasms apiece later, Kelly finally mustered the energy to get up and return the dress to its hanger from where they'd knocked it carelessly to the floor. It probably needed to be ironed now, but that seemed a small price to pay for the pleasure she'd just experienced.

"Seriously, that dress looks way better on you than it ever did on me," Jillian said, as if they hadn't taken a several-hour sex break since starting the dress conversation. "It was my maid of honor dress for Serena's wedding, so I didn't even get to pick the color or anything. It already looks good as is, but you should get it tailored so it's a perfect fit. Are you feeling better about the whole gala thing now?"

Kelly nodded. "Yeah, definitely. Thanks a lot for the dress. I'm still a little nervous about seeing Sarah, though."

"Maybe think of her like a snake or something, which shouldn't be too much of a stretch. She's probably more scared of you than you are of her," Jillian suggested.

"That's awful," Kelly said, laughing.

She curled into Jillian's side as Jillian draped an arm around her. Somehow, the thought of facing Sarah didn't seem quite so daunting with Jillian by her side. As much as she didn't want to admit it to Allison, it did feel like they were going as a couple. She'd never felt so comfortable this quickly with anyone she'd dated before. Or not dated, in this case. Dan hadn't even known she had a sister by this point, let alone her anxieties about her. She'd have to be careful not to let herself get too comfortable and start thinking of it as a real relationship.

❖

Back in her own apartment that night, her new dress stowed safely in her closet, she pondered Jillian's words more seriously. While Sarah wasn't *afraid* of her per se, she'd seemed to be as rattled as Kelly about their chance meeting at the law firm. This time, Kelly had the advantage of near certainty that Sarah would be at the gala. Maybe this was a chance for her to be the bigger person, to give Sarah a heads-up so she wasn't taken completely unaware either. She easily found Sarah's work email address online and drafted a message:

Sarah,

I wanted to let you know I'll be at the gala next week. I imagine I'll see you there.
Kelly

She dithered back and forth for a while but finally pressed send before she could talk herself out of it.

She didn't hear back, but she hadn't expected to. Jillian found her a tailor who could alter the dress in time, and by the day of the gala, she felt as ready for it as she ever would be. Allison came over to help with her hair and makeup. Once she pulled on the perfectly fitting dress, she barely recognized herself in the mirror.

"You look *amazing*," Allison squealed. "Jillian's going to lose her mind."

Kelly brushed off the compliment, but privately, she was hoping so too. Allison tried to linger long enough to overlap with Jillian's arrival, but Kelly was on to her and chivvied her out the door.

"Okay, fine, I'm going, but you can't keep me from meeting her forever," she called over her shoulder as she left.

"Oh, watch me," Kelly yelled at her departing back, grinning. Jillian's attraction to her might have been strong enough to withstand all the embarrassing stories Allison could tell her about their college days, but she wasn't willing to take that risk.

A few minutes later, there was a knock at the door. She pulled it open and was surprised to see Jillian standing there.

"Hi, I thought you were just going to text when you got here. Wow, you look great!" Kelly said. Jillian was wearing a one-shoulder dress in soft pink that hugged her body in all the right places. Her hair was in an updo like the night they'd met, and she had some kind of glittery makeup on that made her look even more luminous than usual.

Jillian just stood there in silence, staring at her.

"Did you...want to come in?" Kelly asked uncertainly.

"What?" Jillian said, "Oh. No, I found a parking spot right out front, and I was just thinking it seemed a little unchivalrous to text you when I could easily come to the door. You look... very nice. That color suits you. Anyway, shall we?"

For all of her insistence to Allison that this wasn't a date, Kelly didn't think it was only her anxiety about seeing Sarah that was giving her butterflies as she and Jillian walked to the car in silence. The night felt potentially momentous, a heady mix of anticipation and the slight fear that she was balancing on the edge of a precipice. She only hoped she was steady enough on her feet not to fall.

CHAPTER TWELVE

Jillian kept stealing glances at Kelly as she drove. When Kelly had opened the door, Jillian had been struck dumb, only able to ogle her like a lovesick teenager with a crush. She hadn't been exaggerating when she'd said the dress looked better on Kelly, but now that it was tailored to her, she was an absolute vision. She was wearing more makeup than usual but just enough to bring out the flecks of green in her eyes. The whole ride over, Jillian had been berating herself for agreeing to go to this stupid thing at all, but now she couldn't remember why she hadn't wanted to go.

She reminded herself that she actually had to get them there safely and forced her attention back on the road. She flexed her hands on the steering wheel, her nerves and dread returning now that she wasn't looking at Kelly. She hadn't mentioned it, but the gala was being held in none other than the same hotel where she'd gotten married ten years ago.

Kelly seemed nervous too, fidgeting with the clasp of her clutch as they pulled up to the front of the hotel. Jillian reached over and patted her thigh right before two valets opened the car doors, and Kelly gave her a small smile.

"I emailed Sarah to tell her I was coming," Kelly said while a doorman ushered them inside.

Jillian raised her eyebrows. "Why? I thought you'd want the element of surprise."

"I did consider that," she admitted. "But then I thought about how much I'd hate having her sprung on me if she knew in advance we'd be in the same place, and I decided it would be nicer to let her know."

Jillian shook her head in wonder. As if she needed any more proof that Kelly was a much better person than she was, there she went showing a level of maturity and empathy Jillian could never match in a thousand years.

"Any last words of advice before we go to the cocktail hour?" Kelly asked nervously.

Jillian snorted derisively. "Don't drink too much, don't talk to anyone for more than five minutes, and kiss as much ass as you can stand to. Oh, and name-drop Harvard and Yale as much as you can. God, I hate these things. I'll see you at dinner."

"Wait, you're not staying with me?" Kelly asked, her eyes panic-stricken.

"I don't know if that's such a good idea," Jillian said, shifting uncomfortably. Most people wouldn't notice if they stayed together while they circulated, but some of her cannier colleagues who knew both of them might. It was one thing to arrive together but quite another to stay by each other's sides all night. The fact that she'd have an infinitely better time if she stayed with Kelly was immaterial.

Kelly looked at her pleadingly. "Jillian, please. At least stay with me until I see where Sarah is so I can avoid her. I don't want her to sneak up on me when I'm by myself."

Knowing it was a mistake even as she did it, Jillian said, "Okay, *fine*, I can't abandon you to that fate. Let's do it."

They made their way into the buzzing crowd. The cocktail reception was being held in a different part of the hotel from the ballroom, and Jillian breathed a quiet sigh of relief that she wouldn't have to deal with an onslaught of wedding memories just yet. She saw Meghan, an old frenemy from law school, who greeted her with overly elaborate air kisses and fake enthusiasm.

"This must be Tessa," Meghan exclaimed, smiling toothily at Kelly. "You look great for your age. I have to know who your surgeon is. And you're awfully tall for a ballerina."

"Um, oh no, I'm not...I'm Kelly. Kelly Lattimore. I work with Jillian," Kelly said.

"Tessa and I split up a few months ago," Jillian said through gritted teeth.

"How devastating, I'm sorry. I had no idea," Meghan said, and Jillian suspected she was lying her perfectly toned ass off. "Nice to meet you, Kelly. *Lattimore*, did you say?"

"Oh, look, there's Tom Sullivan. We've really got to go say hello. Nice to see you, Meghan," Jillian said and yanked Kelly away.

Kelly raised her eyebrows once they were out of Meghan's earshot. "That was...interesting," she said.

"I told you, these things are terrible," Jillian said. "Just make like a shark and keep moving."

They circulated for half an hour or so, Kelly following Jillian's directions to a T. As Jillian suspected, there were a lot of fellow Ivy League alumni among the crowd. Between that and the Lattimore name, she predicted Kelly would have a few dozen new LinkedIn requests the next day.

They had nearly escaped a drunk octogenarian regaling them with stories of his golf prowess when he waved to a passing couple. "Sally, Gordie, get over here and say hello to these lovely young ladies."

"Oh no," Kelly whispered as the elegantly dressed couple approached.

"Hello, Kelly dear. What a lovely dress. We didn't know you'd be here," the woman said cheerfully, her snow-white hair perfectly coifed. After a sideways glance at her husband's stony expression, the smile slid off her face.

"Gordon and Sally Lattimore, may I present...er..." the octogenarian said. He had clearly forgotten their names.

"Jillian Briggs," Jillian said smoothly. "And clearly, you already know Kelly."

"How are you, Gra—Mr. and Mrs. Lattimore?" Kelly muttered.

"Very well, thank you. We've got to be going now," Gordon Lattimore said brusquely, steering his wife away without a backward glance.

Kelly stared at the floor as her grandparents departed while Jillian tried to bore holes in their backs with her glare. *What the ever-loving fuck is wrong with these people.*

They managed to escape their amiable captor, and Jillian tugged Kelly to the edge of the bustling crowd.

"I had no idea they'd be here," Kelly said miserably. "They've been traveling a lot lately, and I thought they were still out of town."

"They make you call them Mr. and Mrs. Lattimore?"

"Only around other people. When it's just us, I can call them Grandmother and Grandfather."

Jillian stared at her incredulously. "Grandmother and Grandfather? Are they from fucking *Little House on the Prairie*? Whatever, that's not even important compared to how shitty that was. God forbid they actually talk to you at all. What absolute assholes."

Kelly's eyes widened earnestly. "Oh no, they're not that bad. Well, Grandmother isn't, anyway. Grandfather's the one who's more worried about people knowing about me. He was really angry when he found out that my mom didn't give me her last name instead. I just hope they didn't think we were *together* together, you know? Maybe I should send them an apology for not checking first to see if they were coming tonight."

Jillian rarely found herself lost for words, but this was one such occasion. If this was how Kelly's grandparents treated her all the time, she was probably better off that they'd ignored her for so much of her life. It infuriated her that Kelly felt the need to apologize for her very existence. So far, the gala ticket she'd won as a reward for her hard work was proving to be more of a curse.

Jillian realized that Kelly's family woes weren't over yet as she caught sight of a familiar blond head nearby. "Sarah at ten o'clock," she murmured to Kelly, who promptly tensed. "Breathe," Jillian instructed, and Kelly drew in a deep breath and exhaled, then resumed breathing normally.

To Jillian's surprise, Sarah was heading toward them purposefully, her fiancé Ted in tow. Now Jillian was feeling tense, too. She doubted Sarah would make a scene at such a big and prominent event, but in her experience, old money rich people were weird and unpredictable, and there was no telling what they'd do. Maybe Sarah had seen the interaction with her grandparents and was going to tell Kelly off for speaking to them or something.

Sarah reached them and stood directly facing Kelly. Jillian could feel Kelly waiting with bated breath for what she'd say. "Hello, Kelly. Hello, Jillian," Sarah said formally, inclining her head to each of them.

Kelly blinked. "Uh, hi, Sarah. Hi, Ted," she said. He nodded back and gave her a small smile.

"I wanted to say thank you for letting me know you'd be here tonight," Sarah said.

Kelly smiled at her hesitantly. "I wasn't sure if I should,

but I just figured if I was in your shoes, I'd at least want to know in advance."

"Well, it was very…decent of you. I wish I'd told you that Grandmother and Grandfather were coming. They're leaving before the dinner, so it didn't even occur to me," Sarah said. She didn't quite smile, but there was an unexpected element of warmth in her voice.

Huh. She calls them that too. What a weird fucking family. Jillian hoped her surprise didn't register on her face. Whatever Kelly had written in her email, it had clearly done a lot to thaw some of the ice between them. Figuring she might as well keep things cordial as long as possible, Jillian asked Sarah how her work at the Lattimore Foundation was going.

"It's been good," Sarah said. "I'm trying to get us to branch out a little beyond our usual areas of focus, but there's some resistance to change on the board."

"That reminds me, do you have anyone at your firm who specializes in animal law?" Ted asked. Sarah shot him a look out of the corner of her eye but didn't say anything.

"Hmm, not that I can think of," Jillian said, running through her mental roster of partners.

"One of my favorite professors from law school does," Kelly said. "I'll send you her contact information. I'm sure she could put you in touch with someone who can help you. What in particular—"

"I'm afraid we've got to get going now," Sarah said, waving at them and pulling Ted away.

"What on earth was that about?" Jillian asked as she and Kelly stared at each other.

Kelly shook her head. "I'm as lost as you are. But I think that was more words in one conversation than she's said to me over the past five years or so, so I'm going to call it a success."

Jillian realized she'd fulfilled her commitment to stay with Kelly until after she'd spoken to Sarah. It would probably be best for them to go their separate ways for the rest of the night, but she found herself reluctant to do so. She wondered if she wasn't being perhaps a tiny bit paranoid and decided it was worth the risk. After all, Kelly was still new to this type of event, and she might continue to need Jillian's guidance. The surprise encounter with her grandparents didn't seem to have rattled her too much, but surely she was still feeling on edge from it. Besides, other than Serena, whom she hadn't been able to locate yet in the crowd, there was no one else here Jillian wanted to talk to anyway. Kelly's presence was the only reason she made it through the rest of the cocktail hour without dying of boredom.

They finally made it into the ballroom where the dinner was being held. They'd been assigned to the same table, which was a relief since Serena was several tables away. At least Jillian would have someone to talk to other than Leon, who was seated across from her. As she laughed at Kelly's impression of one of her law professors, she felt eyes on her and realized Leon was watching them from across the table, an unusually shrewd look on his face. It unsettled her, but he looked away, and she hoped she had just imagined it.

After dinner, she let Kelly pull her onto the dance floor, even though it was also a bad idea. They danced for a few songs before she saw Serena trying to wend her way through the crowd toward them. Serena seemed to be trying to say something, but Jillian couldn't hear her over the music. She pointed at her ear and shrugged while Serena mimed something frantically.

As Serena got closer, she heard her say, "Jillian, I saw—"

"Hi, Jillian," said someone behind her. Ice flooded her veins. She'd have known that voice anywhere.

"Hello, Tessa," she said, turning to face her ex-wife.

Of all the boring work events in all the towns in all the world... Jillian took in the sight of Tessa standing mere feet from her in the very room where they'd celebrated their marriage a decade ago. There were a few streaks of gray in her dark hair, but her eyes were as bright a blue as ever. It was a surreal moment, like no time had passed; for the briefest of flashes, instead of pink and navy blue, they were both in white, preparing for their first dance. Before all the fighting and tears and broken promises, they'd had something real, something worth fighting for. Whether either of them could have done enough to salvage it, they'd never know now.

"You remember Penny," Tessa said, inclining her head to the redheaded woman at her side whose hand she was holding so naturally.

Jillian gritted her teeth and gave Penny the blandest smile she could manage, hoping it didn't look more like a grimace. She didn't have proof, but she'd long suspected Penny and Tessa's relationship had overlapped their marriage by at least a few months.

"Some generous donors gave a few tickets to the symphony, and Penny was lucky enough to snag a couple. I didn't expect you to be here this year. You always hated these things," Tessa said.

"People change," Jillian said with a shrug. "Kelly and I are having a great time. Oh, this is Kelly. Kelly, this is Tessa and Penny." She put a possessive arm around Kelly's waist and drew her close while Kelly shot her an inscrutable look out of the corner of her eye. She had no idea what that was about. Kelly's grandparents were long gone, so it wasn't like they would see and misinterpret.

Tessa's eyebrows rose. "Hi, Kelly. Nice to meet you. How did you two meet?"

"It's, uh, nice to meet you too," Kelly said. "We met at work."

"I suppose you'd have to. It's not like Jillian's ever anywhere else," Tessa said wryly.

Jillian bristled. She was grateful to Kelly for sticking with their cover story, but she felt an insane urge to tell Tessa where they'd really met, just to shut her up about Jillian's work obsession. Instead, she kissed Kelly's cheek and said, "Oh, Kelly's very good at getting me out of the office. We went up to the cabin last month, no work allowed. You loved it, didn't you, Kelly?"

Kelly was giving her that cryptic look again, but she nodded. "Yeah, it was great."

"Well, that sounds very nice," Tessa said dubiously. "Pen, that's the place I told you about, the very…*rustic* place. Anyway, we won't keep you, I just thought we'd say hi."

As Jillian watched them depart, Serena finally fought her way through the crowd of dancers and reached them. "Ugh, this place is a madhouse. I swear it took me five minutes to move about twenty feet. I was trying to warn you she was here, but obviously, I was too late," she said, panting.

"It fucking figures she'd be here," Jillian grumbled.

"I see she's still with the side chick," Serena said darkly.

"Guess so," Jillian said with a shrug. If she acted like she didn't care for long enough, maybe eventually, she wouldn't. "Oh, did you see Meghan? Kelly and I ran into her during the cocktail hour, and she thought Kell—hey, where'd she go?"

Kelly, who had been stuck to her side like glue all night, had vanished. She looked through the swarms of people for the distinctive pale green dress, but it was nowhere to be seen. Kelly was gone.

CHAPTER THIRTEEN

Jillian hadn't even noticed her leaving the gala after that little performance for Tessa, which frustrated Kelly but didn't surprise her. She spent Saturday morning rage-cleaning her apartment, scouring the bathroom grout until her fingers cramped and arguing with Jillian in her head. Whatever comfort she'd gotten from Jillian's presence during her interactions with her family had been obliterated by the way Jillian had trotted her out in front of Tessa like some dumb prize she'd won at a fair. If she could just find the right words, maybe she could make imaginary Jillian understand how cheap and used she'd felt.

Once there wasn't a speck of dust or grime anywhere in her apartment, she rode the commuter rail to her mom's apartment, ignoring Jillian's calls and leaving her texts on read. She felt like a little kid just wanting to hide behind her mom and have her make everything okay.

They lounged on the couch all day, watching Lifetime movies and eating junk food for dinner. The sharp rush of anger slowly softened into a thudding ache that felt annoyingly close to sadness instead. Her mom didn't press her on what had happened, and Kelly didn't feel like talking about it until Sunday afternoon.

"It just sucks that she's the one who's been all, 'we have to keep it a secret,' and, 'we're not dating,' and then, she's treating me like her trophy girlfriend in front of half the firm just to make her ex jealous."

Her mom nodded sympathetically. "It was a lousy thing to do. Understandable in the situation—she's only human—but still lousy. I guess the question now is, what do you want to do about it?"

Kelly sighed. "I don't know," she said at last. "Before Friday night, I would've said everything was great as it was. But it made me feel…manipulated, I guess. Like she didn't even see me as a person, just something she could use."

"I hope you know I support you, whatever you end up doing," her mom said. "I don't care if your grandparents have a problem with it."

Kelly tossed a handful of peanut butter M&M's into her mouth and chewed them while she collected her thoughts. "I think the worst part is that I kind of *liked* it when she was acting like we were really together," she admitted. It wasn't a pleasant realization, but she'd been analyzing her own reaction since the gala, and the inevitable conclusion was that she'd come down with a case of feelings for Jillian. She should have known better, that it would be impossible for her to keep sex and romantic attachment separate forever.

It couldn't have come at a worse time, either, not when they'd finally hit a balance of discretion that was working for both of them. She wasn't delusional enough to think Jillian might ever feel the same way; she had no interest in a relationship, and she'd been clear about that from the start. Kelly realized she had two choices: end it or continue as they'd been doing and repress her feelings as much as possible.

The decision was easy once she really thought about it. She thought she'd hidden it well, but she'd been miserable when she'd called a halt to things before. She'd still be pining for Jillian either way, so she might as well continue getting some really great sex out of it. That was, if Jillian was still open to that after Kelly had run away from the gala and ignored her all weekend.

On the train back to her apartment, she texted Jillian that she'd been sick and had spent the weekend recuperating at her mom's but would see her at work tomorrow. Jillian responded in less than a minute with a thumbs-up emoji and nothing else. Kelly sighed and shoved her phone into her pocket. Jillian wasn't typically a verbose texter, but it would have been nice for her to say something, anything at all, about Kelly finally resurfacing. It was like she didn't care at all, which, Kelly reminded herself, she didn't. If their arrangement was going to keep working, she'd do well to remember that.

❖

As soon as she got to work on Monday morning, Kelly could tell something was up. The floor was buzzing with conversation when she got off the elevator, but as soon as the clusters of people saw her, they quieted and stared as she walked by. She ignored it as best she could, but she felt dread in the pit of her stomach. She had a feeling she knew what all the whispering and staring was about. She looked across the floor and saw Ezra studying her from a distance. He smiled at her and then picked up his phone. She wasn't surprised to see Jillian emerge from her office moments later. A hush fell over the floor as Jillian walked by.

"Don't you people have work you should be doing?" Jillian barked, and everyone hurriedly returned to their desks, hoping to avoid her wrath. "Hi," Jillian said rather breathlessly when she reached Kelly.

Kelly felt a swell of stupid, hopeless longing at the sight of her but tamped down on it ruthlessly. Jillian would never reciprocate, and she couldn't afford to forget that. "Hi," Kelly said. "I take it everyone knows now?"

"It seems so," Jillian said glumly. "I knew I shouldn't have let you talk me into staying with you during the cocktail hour. Oh well, it was only a matter of time."

Kelly gaped at her, too outraged to speak for a moment. "You think this is *my* fault? You don't think it had more to do with your little dog and pony show for Tessa?" she snapped.

Jillian bit her lip. "Well, that might have had something to do with it."

"I think it had *everything* to do with it," Kelly insisted. At least her mounting irritation was distracting her from her unrequited feelings. "I was fine just walking around talking to people with you. I didn't even touch you when we were dancing. You were the one who was all over me. I had just as much at stake as you, if not more. What if my grandparents had seen us?"

"Okay, fine, maybe you're right," Jillian admitted. "Oh, great," she muttered, looking over Kelly's shoulder.

"I didn't think it was true, but Jillian just admitted someone else was right, so it must be," Leon boomed from behind Kelly. He must have emerged from his office without either of them noticing. "Oh dear, have I interrupted a lovers' quarrel? Kelly, do remember you can't bill the time you spend talking to your girlfriend." He smirked and walked away before either of them could respond.

"Ooh, I hate that man," Jillian muttered, clenching her fists.

Kelly bit the inside of her cheek to keep from grinning at the expression on Jillian's face, reminding herself of how angry and hurt she'd been all weekend. They might not be in a real relationship, but Jillian didn't deserve to be let off the hook too easily.

"Did you need something? I have a lot of work to do," she said as she unlocked her office.

Jillian followed her inside but left the door open. Through the glass walls, Kelly could see faces watching them from around the floor. She hoped they could have a real conversation at some point about what had happened at the gala, but this clearly wasn't the time.

"I was thinking, if we're going to have to deal with all of this no matter what...want to stay over tonight?" Jillian glanced around, then leaned in and whispered "I got some new toys just for you."

Kelly stared at her. *Is she seriously going to act like she did nothing wrong?* "My caseload is pretty high right now. I'll let you know later if I can make it."

"Oh," Jillian said, a flash of surprise in her eyes. That was clearly not the answer she'd expected. "I guess I'll see you later, then. Or maybe not. Just, uh, let me know. Or tell Ezra."

She left Kelly's office, and Kelly tried and failed not to watch her ass as she walked away. The momentary satisfaction she felt at seeing Jillian so taken aback didn't even last until Jillian stuck her head back in.

"On second thought, definitely don't tell Ezra. You can just tell me directly."

"Will do," Kelly said in as bored a tone as she could manage. She could feel Jillian watching her, but she kept her eyes on her still-dark computer screen until Jillian departed.

She threw herself into the heavy Monday morning workload, trying not to think about Jillian. She'd decide how to handle that situation later. She knew she should congratulate herself on holding strong, but it didn't feel like much of a victory when all she wanted was for Jillian to come back.

CHAPTER FOURTEEN

Jillian wondered if Kelly was still feeling sick from whatever bug she'd caught over the weekend. Either that or she was taking the whole secrecy thing way too seriously now that the cat was out of the bag. She didn't know what else could have caused Kelly's icy behavior that morning. As if the day weren't bad enough already, Ezra stopped her before she could enter her office.

"Tessa's here," he whispered. "I put her in there so Kelly wouldn't see her."

"Great, that's just what I need."

"I can ask her to leave if you'd prefer," he said. "If I'd known about you and Kelly sooner, I would have done that right away. I only heard about it this morning from Stacy in the mail room, who heard about it from Mr. Marsh's assistant."

"I swear, this time, I'm really going to kill Leon. The way gossip flies around this place is ridiculous. Wait, I thought you and Stacy weren't friends anymore."

"We aren't," he said darkly. "She knows what she did. This was a bit of a peace offering, I guess. Or more likely, she thought I'd have juicy details for her. Do you want me to try to get Tessa out of here?"

"No, it's fine," she said with an exasperated sigh. "It'll be easier to get rid of her if I talk to her first and probably faster than you trying to get her to leave."

She glanced across the floor. Kelly was watching her, but as soon as she saw Jillian looking, she went back to staring at her computer screen. Jillian hoped Ezra had been successful at stowing Tessa in her office before Kelly had noticed her. If Kelly had seen her, maybe that was another reason she was acting so withdrawn this morning.

Jillian steeled herself, then walked into her office. "What do you want?" she asked without preamble.

"Hello to you too, Jillian. I'm well, thanks so much for asking." Tessa stood looking out at the city, her back to the door.

"I really don't have time for your bullshit today," Jillian snipped. Half her mind was busy wondering if Kelly would be coming over later, the other half worrying about professional fallout.

"It's always such a pleasure to see you. How I've missed this," Tessa said, finally turning. Irritatingly, she still moved as gracefully as she had when she was still dancing. Jillian wondered if she saw this as a performance too.

"Get to the point and get out," Jillian said.

"There's no need to be so belligerent. I didn't actually come here to argue with you."

Jillian tapped her foot impatiently, the effect lessened by the carpet muffling the sound of her shoe.

Tessa gave her a long look, then sighed. "Fine. I can tell you don't want me here."

"You're quite the mind reader. And here I thought I was being subtle," Jillian said nastily.

"Penny and I are getting married."

"You...what?" Her brain short-circuited as she tried to process Tessa's words.

"It'll be announced in the *Globe* this week, but I wanted you to hear it from me," Tessa said placidly, as if Jillian hadn't spoken. "I figured I owe you that much."

Jillian forced her face into a robotic grin. "Already? Congratulations. What a fast courtship. You can't have been together for very long."

Tessa ignored the implication. "Thank you, we're very excited. If you'll give me your new address, I'll send you and Carrie a save-the-date."

"It's Kelly," Jillian said through gritted teeth. As if she was going to sit through Tessa and Penny's stupid wedding. Even Kelly's presence couldn't salvage that into something worth enduring.

"Kelly, that's right. Or I suppose I can just send it here, since you're both in the office so much," Tessa said with a tinkling laugh.

Jillian was impressed with her own fortitude as she made the usual inquiries about venue—another hotel ballroom—and season—winter, the perfect timing for their ski resort honeymoon—and pretended to admire the ring—understated, yet clearly expensive. She couldn't have cared less about any of it, but she'd rather die than let Tessa see how rattled she was by the news. By the time she led Tessa to the door, discreetly checking that Kelly wasn't watching them from her desk, her pulse had skyrocketed, and she was wondering if it was possible to fake smile her way into a stroke.

"Is Callie on this floor too?" Tessa asked, looking around at the nearby cubicles.

"Don't even think about talking to her." Jillian didn't bother to correct her again on Kelly's name. Tessa was obviously there to try to mess with her head, and the best way to win mind games was not to play.

"What?" Tessa widened her eyes innocently. "I'd much rather us be friends than enemies, Jillian."

"I have zero interest in being friends with you," Jillian said, jabbing the elevator button harder, as if that would make it arrive faster. If she could just get Tessa out of there without running into Kelly, she'd be in the clear. That had been uncomfortable enough at the gala, and she wasn't eager to repeat the experience.

"I still care about you as a person, you know," Tessa said as the elevator finally arrived and began disgorging passengers.

"Sure you do," Jillian said, checking that the coast was clear.

"I'm serious. Why else would I have come here to tell you this in person and put myself through your hostility?"

"To see if I'd beg you to come back?" Jillian mused. "To rub it in my face? To try to fuck with Kelly and me? I can think of a bunch more reasons why you didn't just send a text if you'd like me to continue."

Tessa rolled her eyes, a note of irritation finally creeping into her voice. "Just because that would be your motivation doesn't mean it's mine. Tell Kelly I said hello and to keep an eye out for that save-the-date card."

To Jillian's ire, the elevator doors slid closed with Tessa getting the last word. She fumed all the way back to her office, wishing she could call Tessa back upstairs so she could deliver the perfect verbal coup de grace. At least she'd goaded her into showing her annoyance by the end.

"I think Kelly's been in with Mr. Marsh since before Tessa left," Ezra muttered when she returned. "I was only away from my desk for a minute."

At least one thing had gone right today. Hopefully, that trend would continue, and Kelly would agree to come over tonight. Maybe she should send flowers to Kelly's office to try to entice her. No, that would attract even more attention and stir the rumors into a frenzy, not to mention possibly give Kelly the wrong idea. She'd have to think of something else.

❖

"Get this, then she invited us to her wedding. It's pathetic how she came here trying to act like she doesn't care what I think when you know the whole thing was so she could watch my reaction," Jillian ranted to Serena over lunch. Kelly had been bustling around the office all morning, and it had been impossible to pin her down for even the briefest conversation.

"'Us' meaning?" Serena said, her brow furrowed.

"Kelly and me."

"That's a relief. I was afraid you meant you and me," Serena said.

Jillian chuckled at the thought. "No, you're off the hook. Although I'm sure I could wrangle you an invite if you and Mike want to come gawk at the spectacle with us."

Serena stared at her. "You can't possibly be planning to go."

"My first thought was hell no, but I bet I could convince Kelly to go with me. There's nothing like showing up to your ex's wedding with a hot date to win the breakup."

"Wow." Serena crumpled up her napkin and tossed it onto her empty plate. "For someone so smart, you're doing an awfully good impression of an idiot."

"What are you talking about? It's basically a foolproof plan."

"First of all, you'd be doing exactly what you just accused Tessa of."

"Hey!" Jillian protested.

"Don't bullshit me, you know it's true. But let's set that aside for a moment. More importantly, how do you think it would make Kelly feel?"

"I...hadn't even thought about that," Jillian said sheepishly.

"No kidding," Serena said with a dismissive snort. "I like that girl, and I don't want you screwing things up this early in the game."

"That implies that you think I'm inevitably going to screw things up at some point."

"I plead the Fifth. I have a meeting coming up, I'll see you later."

Jillian scowled at Serena's newly vacant seat. Surely, Kelly would understand, right? If she looked at it from a certain angle, it was even flattering that Jillian wanted to show her off. Serena had gotten into her head, though, and it no longer seemed that simple. She imagined if Kelly wanted her to tag along to some event to make Dan jealous, and it certainly didn't feel like a compliment. That settled it. Tessa's save-the-date card was going right where it belonged, in the garbage. Feeling freer already, she dug into work while she waited to hear from Kelly.

The rest of the day dragged on interminably. Every time Jillian left her office, she felt the attention of everyone nearby as they hastily pretended they hadn't been staring at her door. People she barely knew "just happened to drop by for a chat," which was irritating on its own but also made it impossible to get any work done. An overgrown frat bro partner she usually avoided at all costs offered her a high five after a meeting. She stared at him, stone-faced, until his hand wilted back to his side, and he scurried away, muttering something about needing to call a client.

By the time evening rolled around, her jaw ached from

clenching her teeth so tightly, and her nerves were as taut as bowstrings. A night spent dominating Kelly sounded like the perfect way to take the edge off, but she still hadn't heard a peep from her about their evening plans. Reluctant though she was to risk drawing more notice by spending time together at work, she asked Kelly if she wanted to have dinner together via the firm's messaging app. After a longer delay than usual, Kelly agreed. It was probably pathetic how happy it made her, but she tried not to think too hard about what that meant.

CHAPTER FIFTEEN

Serena stopped by Kelly's office after lunch, offering her support and assuring her that the gossip mill would soon wear itself out. Kelly hoped she was right; aside from anything else, it was hard to concentrate on her work when she kept feeling people's eyes on her from nearby desks. She needed her wits about her now more than ever. As she and Jillian had feared, Leon was using their connection as an excuse to be even tougher on her than before. She accepted his biting criticisms without complaint and logged her hours scrupulously, not wanting to give him anything legitimate to point to about her work performance. He kept her so busy with research and redoing memos she'd already drafted that she hardly had to put any effort into avoiding Jillian.

She knew giving Jillian the silent treatment was probably childish, but it was self-protection as much as anything else. She didn't trust herself not to give in and accept Jillian's non-apology, and she deserved better than that. Even a token gesture on Jillian's part would have to be good enough for now. It came in the form of a dinner invitation, and she seized on it eagerly. She had enough respect for herself to wait a few minutes before responding and was gratified by Jillian's rare usage of an exclamation point when she replied, *Great!*

Their dinner conversation stayed light, mostly on their current cases and what movies they would've liked to see if they hadn't been working all the time. Jillian didn't bring up the gala or unfairly blaming Kelly for their secret getting out, but Kelly didn't really expect her to. Jillian still wanted to be seen with her around the office now that people knew, and that would have to be enough.

All the inner turmoil of the last few days felt worth it that night when she fell asleep in Jillian's bed after several rounds of outrageously good sex, even by her now-elevated standards. She woke up in the middle of the night to Jillian prodding her.

"Kelly? Are you awake?" Jillian whispered.

"I am now," she mumbled, trying and probably failing not to sound as grumpy as she felt.

"I'm sorry," Jillian said.

"For waking me up?" Kelly asked.

She could see Jillian shake her head in the faint glow that snuck in from the city lights outside the window. "Well, that too. But I meant for everything with Tessa at the gala. I didn't...I didn't handle that well. At all. I shouldn't have treated you that way."

Kelly was on the verge of saying it was okay, but something stopped her. Instead, she said, "No, you shouldn't have. It was shitty. So was blaming me for everyone finding out."

She could hear the wince in Jillian's voice as she replied, "You're right. I really am sorry about all of it. Tessa stopped by this morning to try to rub her happiness in my face, and I realized that's exactly what I was trying to do with you. You don't deserve that."

"Oh yeah, the girl who dropped off my mail said something about your ex being here, but I didn't know if she was just confused."

"Fucking Stacy," Jillian grumbled. "Whatever, that's not even relevant. Is there something I can do to make it up to you?"

The true answer, *say you've fallen for me too*, wasn't something she could ask for, so instead, Kelly said, "It's okay. Just don't do it again."

"I won't," Jillian promised, planting a kiss on her shoulder. "And let's say I owe you a favor or big gesture to be called in later."

"I'll hold you to that," Kelly warned her, smiling into the dark.

❖

Kelly hoped Serena's prediction would come true sooner rather than later. If people were losing interest in her and Jillian's ersatz relationship, she certainly couldn't tell yet. Her fellow first-year associates seemed to have divided themselves into two camps. Half of them seemed to feel that Jillian's menacing aura now extended to Kelly too, treating her with a level of deference usually reserved for partners. The rest had swung in the opposite direction, openly gawking when she walked past or slyly asking about her weekend plans. More than once, she had entered the break room only for the chatter to drop off immediately as everyone loudly started discussing the weather. She didn't know for a fact that she and Jillian had been the previous topic of conversation, but the knowing looks from some of the group told her plenty.

The one exception was Madison Shafer, who was also dating a partner. She jokingly thanked Kelly for taking the attention off her and Alex before commiserating and mentioning that she'd started interviewing at other firms. She was getting tired of subtle remarks about how lucky she was to be assigned such good cases, even though she'd earned them.

"Besides, I don't know if Big Law's for me, anyway," she confided. "I'm feeling really drawn to immigration law, and I don't get to do any of that here. I'm meeting with a boutique firm next week that specializes in it."

Kelly wished her good luck, slightly envious that Madison had the option of leaving for a much less lucrative specialty. She felt a twinge of unease that Jillian had been right about Madison leaving, even if her relationship wasn't the only reason. Hopefully, there would be new grist for the rumor mill soon, before Jillian started freaking out.

Ezra was a big fan of Killian, as he called them; he managed to carve out at least fifteen minutes a day when free time in both of their schedules overlapped and they could grab a cup of coffee together. Leon continued to be more demanding than ever, but she and Jillian spent so much time laughing at him about it behind his back that it didn't even bother her anymore.

She emailed Sarah the name of her law professor like she'd said she would and was shocked to receive a reply a few days later both thanking her and inviting her out for coffee. She wondered vaguely if Sarah was planning to poison her, but her curiosity was strong enough to make the risk seem worth it.

"Thank you for meeting me," Sarah said primly once they were seated in the bougie coffeehouse she'd suggested.

"Sure," Kelly said. "I admit, I was a little surprised about the invitation."

Sarah fiddled with the handle of her espresso cup and avoided Kelly's eyes. "I met with Professor Gardner. She was very helpful and gave me a number of useful contacts."

"I'm glad."

"She spoke very highly of you," Sarah said, finally looking up. "She said you were one of the brightest students she's ever had and one of the nicest too."

"Um, that's very nice of her," Kelly said, feeling more baffled by the second. "Look, Sarah, I have to ask, what's this all about? Normally, you avoid me like the plague, so what's changed?"

Sarah sighed. "I…it's going to sound stupid."

"I'm sure it won't," Kelly said, eager for her to get to the point.

"Promise you won't laugh?" Sarah demanded. When Kelly nodded, she said, "Okay, fine. The truth is, my dog died about a month ago."

Kelly stared at her, nonplussed. "I'm sorry to hear that. But what does that have to do with…this?" she said, gesturing between them.

Sarah twisted her engagement ring around and around on her finger. "Ranger was the best dog ever. He was my best friend. I loved him so much, and now he's just…gone." Tears glistened in her eyes as she continued, "Believe me, I know how silly this sounds, but losing him made me realize how short life is, and do I really want to hold on to a grudge for the sake of it? Ted thought it might help me to reach out to you. After all, you're the only sister I have."

Kelly managed not to say *as far as we know, anyway*, since their father's infidelities were doubtless a touchy subject. She wasn't really sure how to respond. This was the most openly emotional conversation she'd ever had with Sarah. Finally, she said, "Ranger sounds really great. What kind of dog was he?"

"He was a pit bull, a rescue. He'd been used as a bait dog in fighting rings before he was rescued. Even with everything he went through, he was just the most loving animal," Sarah said tremulously. "Anyway, I decided I want to do more in animal rights advocacy. I've been trying to get the Lattimore Foundation involved, but that's been a no go so far. Ted and I are looking into starting our own nonprofit instead. That's why I need animal law experts."

"Wow," Kelly said. "That's amazing. Poor Ranger. That's a great way to honor his memory. Can I see a picture of him?"

That had been the right question to ask because Sarah lit up like a Christmas tree and proceeded to show her several dozen pictures. "I was always jealous of you, you know," Sarah said quietly as she put her phone away.

"What? You were jealous of *me*? Why?" Kelly's jaw actually fell open.

Sarah smiled humorlessly. "My parents…they hate each other. I'm pretty sure they only stay together out of spite to make each other miserable. I could always tell when Dad had come back from seeing your mom. He was actually happy for a change."

"Huh," Kelly said, mulling over Sarah's words. She thought about what she remembered of her own parents' interactions before her dad had vanished from her life for the rest of her childhood. She could see what Sarah meant. Even though he rarely came over more than one night a week, her dad had always seemed happy and relaxed at their house. He'd bring Kelly's mom flowers and often candy or a toy for Kelly. After dinner, her parents sometimes danced around the living room, cheek to cheek, until her father's phone buzzed, and he took off in a hurry. Compared to how Sarah described her own household, it sounded like paradise.

"And Grandmother and Grandfather go on about you all the time," Sarah said bitterly. "They think you walk on water or something. I don't…I didn't get why you always had to do what I did a year or two later, just so they could tell me how much better you were at it than me. You couldn't let me have even one thing to myself."

"Are you serious?" Kelly exclaimed. "They've always compared me to you. Everything I ever did, they wanted me to do because you'd done it first. My mom had no money for sleepaway camps or tennis lessons or art classes. I only did that stuff because that's what they'd pay for. And they'd always talk about how great *you* were at whatever it was."

Sarah snorted. "That's news to me. You should've heard them when you got into Yale. They wouldn't stop saying how smart you were and how resourceful you were to get all those scholarships."

"Oh, that's nice. Really nice," Kelly said sarcastically. "The only reason I had to do all of that is that neither they nor Benton would pitch in a cent. And they certainly weren't running over to hug me at that stupid gala. Maybe they finally got tired of pitting us against each other and decided to pick you."

"They have a funny way of showing it. They all but said I only got in because of my mother. You know the Hillerton Concert Hall they built a few years before I started there? Her maiden name is Hillerton," Sarah explained. "And it's not like I got the job I have now on merit."

"Wow, what an awful thing to say to anyone, let alone your own grandchild," Kelly said, righteous anger rising on Sarah's behalf.

Sarah made a dismissive movement too elegant to be called a shrug. "I suppose they were just trying to push me to be better, but it probably wasn't the best way to go about it."

"No kidding," Kelly said. "Well, I think it's bullshit. Fuck all that."

Sarah looked shocked, but a nervous giggle escaped. "You're right. It *is* bullshit." She said it carefully, like she'd never said the word before. For all Kelly knew, she hadn't.

"Maybe we could start over? Get to know each other on our own terms?" Kelly suggested.

"I'd like that. I'd like that very much," Sarah said, a smile slowly taking over her face. "You know, they do serve lunch here…"

By the time Kelly had to leave to return to the office, they'd hesitantly agreed to meet up again in a few weeks. She could hardly believe it.

Neither could Jillian when she filled her in on it later. "Are you sure this isn't some kind of trick?" she asked.

"I don't see how it could be," Kelly said. "She wasn't asking me for anything."

"Hmm, I don't know. Maybe she needs a kidney, and she's buttering you up before she asks."

Kelly laughed and shook her head. "You weren't there. She seemed really genuine."

"Of course she did, she needs your kidney," Jillian said teasingly.

"Well, I'll tell you one thing, she really loved that dog. She had thousands of pictures of him on her phone. You can't fake that level of devotion," Kelly said. "I feel bad for her, actually. She was so sad when she talked about losing him. Even all the money and power and connections in the world can't do anything to help that."

Jillian smiled at her and shook her head. "You're a wonder, Kelly Lattimore," she said softly.

Kelly felt herself blushing under Jillian's scrutiny. "Why?"

"You just are, that's all," Jillian said. "Anyway, I have a client meeting now. See you at my place tonight?"

CHAPTER SIXTEEN

Now that there was no need to hide anymore, Kelly started staying over four or five nights a week. Sometimes they didn't have sex if one or both of them was too exhausted from their long days at the office. The process was insidious, inch by inch. It wasn't until Kelly asked hesitantly if Jillian would mind setting aside some space in the closet for her work clothes that Jillian even realized what was happening, how accustomed she was becoming to Kelly's presence.

She said yes but begged off having Kelly over for the next week as the panic set in. The more Kelly wanted from her, the more likely it was that Jillian would let her down. She couldn't go through that again, not with someone she cared about as much as Kelly.

Kelly seemed to take the hint; at any rate, she didn't bring it up again and continued keeping an extra suit at her desk instead.

They'd never discussed any limits on what they were doing, and once again, Jillian toyed with the idea of broadening her horizons. For all she knew, Kelly might have been doing the same. Well, probably not because she worked even more than Jillian, but theoretically, she could have been. She certainly *should* have been keeping her eggs in more than just the one obviously flawed, Jillian-shaped basket.

As she reflected on what a bizarre path her thoughts had taken, Jillian realized Ezra had been talking to her and was now waiting for her reply. "What was that?" she asked.

"Kelly's birthday is coming up in a few weeks. If you know where you want to take her, I can make reservations. And have you bought her a gift yet?" he said.

Oh no. She'd never corrected the impression that they were in a real relationship, even to Ezra. He'd gotten too invested in it, declaring them his OTP, whatever that meant, and she didn't have it in her to burst his bubble. She had always relied on his help for Tessa's birthday and their anniversary, so it made sense for him to bring it up now when he thought she had a girlfriend.

"I've got it handled," she told him. He nodded skeptically and left her office.

She hemmed and hawed. Doing something big felt distinctively girlfriend-like, but she didn't like the thought of Kelly having a disappointing birthday. But of course, she reminded herself, Kelly had a whole life outside of her: her mom, Dan, Allison, and her other friends. Surely, she'd rather spend it with them anyway, no matter how much Jillian might like the idea of being the one to make it special for her.

She pushed the thought aside and turned her attention back to work for a while, but it wasn't long before Kelly herself was knocking on the door. "I'm having dinner at Sarah and Ted's. Want to come?" she asked.

Jillian smiled. "Do you need me there as a bodyguard?"

"No," Kelly said, rolling her eyes. "We've met up a couple times now. It's actually been sort of...fun. They've been making some headway on their nonprofit thing, and they wanted to talk to you about licensing and stuff. Since I was going over there anyway, I thought maybe we could just go together. Come on, you've got to eat *somewhere*."

❖

Jillian drove them to Sarah and Ted's luxurious townhouse, not far from the firm.

"Whoa," Kelly said as they pulled up, her eyes going wide.

"This makes my old house look like a dump," Jillian said, impressed against her will.

Sarah ushered them inside when they rang the bell. It was the first time Jillian had seen her smile at Kelly, and it made the resemblance between the two of them more striking. They were still a little stilted and awkward, but the tension of their previous encounters had mostly disappeared. Ted was genial and friendly, helping to smooth over the occasional long silences in Kelly and Sarah's conversation.

Jillian noticed what looked like family photos along one wall and wandered over to take a look. It really was amazing how much Kelly and Sarah looked alike. If she hadn't known better, she'd have sworn they were pictures of a young Kelly. She was surprised to see one of Kelly and Sarah together as teenagers. They stood next to each other, Sarah with her arms folded and a sullen expression on her face as Kelly smiled nervously at the camera.

"That was the year we went to summer camps on the same lake," Kelly said.

Sarah laughed. "Oh man, it was like *The Parent Trap*. People kept confusing us. We had to take that picture together just to prove there were two of us. My mom was so mad when she found out about it. She always freaks out whenever anyone mentions you."

Awkward silence descended. "Who's ready to eat?" Ted said loudly.

Every room they saw after dinner contained multiple photos of the late Ranger. As Jillian was walking back to the living room from the powder room—which featured custom wallpaper plastered with Ranger's face—she heard a mewling noise from behind a closed door in the hallway. She pressed her ear to the door, mildly concerned.

"That's our foster kitten room," Ted said, startling her. "We're past kitten season, but they still trickle in occasionally. We've got a litter right now."

"Wow, I didn't know you had cats, too," Jillian said.

"Oh yes," Sarah said as she and Kelly had joined them. "Ranger loved cats, especially kittens. He helped us socialize them. Come see." She led the way into the kitten room and pointed at a large photo on the wall of Ranger lying on the floor covered with kittens. One was lying between his front paws as he licked its head.

"Aww," Kelly exclaimed. She was peering into what looked like a baby's playpen. "Jillian, you have to see them!"

Jillian walked over and joined her. Three kittens were frolicking, although they paused to look up and stare back at Jillian and Kelly. Two were gray with stripes, and one was bright orange. Jillian felt her face break out into a smile against her will. "They *are* cute," she admitted.

"Are either of you interested in adoption?" Sarah asked. "The grays are both girls, and the orange is a boy. They're old enough to go to their forever homes now."

"I wish I could," Kelly said, sounding genuinely sad. "My apartment doesn't allow pets, though. Jillian?"

"Oh no," she said, horrified at the thought. "I'm not a pet person. I don't have time for a pet, anyway."

"Cats don't take a lot of time," Sarah said.

"I'm hardly ever home," Jillian protested.

"They're very self-sufficient," Ted chimed in.

"Come on, Kelly, you know me. Can you imagine me with a cat?" Jillian asked, needing someone to see reason.

"That closet off your hallway would be the perfect spot for a litter box," Kelly said traitorously.

Sarah reached into the playpen and picked up the orange kitten. "Here," she said, thrusting it at Jillian.

She took it instinctively. It squirmed a little, then settled in her hands and started purring. She looked down at it. It looked up at her. "I guess I have a cat now," she said.

She and Kelly stopped at a pet store on the way home to get all the things Bob the kitten would need. Sarah had packed him into a cardboard carrier before Jillian even knew what was happening. She set him up in her guest room first, but he cried endlessly until she opened the door. He seemed happy to have the run of the apartment, exploring every nook and cranny before clawing his way up the couch and settling between her and Kelly.

"I don't know how I let the three of you bamboozle me into this," Jillian grumbled. "I don't know the first thing about taking care of a cat."

"I'll help you," Kelly said earnestly, petting Bob's fuzzy little head as he tried to grab her fingers. "My mom always has at least one or two cats. I miss being around them more often."

Jillian shook her head in disgust. "You know, you and Sarah

are more alike than I expected. You've both got the bleeding heart thing going on, and you're both utterly unwilling to stop until you get what you want."

Kelly smiled. "I *have* been praised for my persistence before. Get it? *Purr*sistence?"

Jillian groaned. "You're officially the worst."

"That's not what you said last night," Kelly said, raising an eyebrow.

Jillian shot her a dirty look, but she had no rejoinder. They'd really outdone themselves the night before, and she might have called Kelly the best and amazing and a lot of other things it was difficult to say to her when she had full control of her faculties, even if they were true.

She ended up having to corral Bob in the guest room again once they moved into the bedroom. It was a little hard to tie Kelly up when he kept pouncing on the rope and trying to fight it. She and Kelly were giggling too much at the sight to stay in the mood, either.

She let him out afterward, and he promptly curled up on the bed contentedly. It was adorable until five in the morning, when he seemed to decide they were sleeping far too late and screamed in their faces for breakfast. She and Kelly had breakfast themselves not long after, unable to fall back asleep.

"So," she said, dangling a cat toy for Bob to chase. "It's almost your birthday."

"I know it is," Kelly said, glancing up from her oatmeal.

Jillian studiously kept her gaze on Bob's tiny feet frantically kicking at the toy as she asked, "Got any plans?"

"I'm going to my mom's the weekend before, and she's going to make all my favorite foods, then Allison is throwing a little get-together the day of. Do you…maybe want to come?" Kelly asked.

Jillian wasn't sure if she meant to her mom's house or to

Allison's party, but the idea of either was equally terrifying. She'd thought of an alternative, though. "I don't think I'll be able to, but how about something the weekend after? It'll be freezing, but we could go up to the cabin again. Or just out to dinner or whatever. You should choose."

She'd worried the cabin might be a sensitive topic after the debacle at the gala, but Kelly's face lit up at the suggestion. "Oh, I'd love to go back there," she said enthusiastically.

Jillian found herself beaming back, disproportionately happy about Kelly's reaction. "Great. I can't promise I won't have to bring some work with me, but I'll do my best to be utterly at your service. Anything you want, just name it."

Kelly's smile flickered so quickly, Jillian would have missed it if she didn't find Kelly's smiles so unfairly transfixing. She regained it quickly, though, and said, "That sounds really great."

Jillian wondered what that was about, but Bob decided her leg was more interesting than the toy and was now trying to climb it, and she got distracted. "This is your fault, you know," she scolded Kelly as she gently freed his claws from her flesh, wincing. "You had to suggest naming him after a mass murderer. Of course he decided to choose violence."

"Whoa, back off," Kelly said, widening her eyes innocently. "There are lots of Bobs! Maybe I suggested it because of Bob...Dole."

Jillian laughed so loudly it startled Bob, who promptly sank his claws into her leg again. "Yes, I'm sure someone born in the late nineties is a *huge* Bob Dole fan. I can't believe that's the first Bob you thought of."

"Okay, maybe Bob Dylan would have been a better example," Kelly said with a giggle.

"Or Bob the Builder," suggested Jillian.

"How about Bob Marley?" Kelly said.

"Or Sideshow Bob. That's also a violent namesake," Jillian said.

"Silent Bob," Kelly said.

Jillian picked Bob up and looked at him sternly. "I *wish* I'd named you after Silent Bob. Then maybe you wouldn't go waking us up so early." He looked back at her innocently, and she felt her heart melt. She pressed him to her chest and kissed the top of his head, then set him down on the floor to scamper away. God help her, she loved the little troublemaker already.

❖

Kelly was over so often in the days following Bob's arrival that Jillian finally gave in to the inevitable and cleared out a foot of closet space and a drawer in the dresser for her. She didn't make a big deal about it, just mentioned it while they were brushing their teeth one night, but Kelly's eyes shone as she thanked her, and Jillian noticed she kept looking over at the empty spot in the closet.

The sight sent a pang through her, and she feared she was making a horrible mistake. She knew she was difficult to live with, alternately distant and overly demanding; Tessa had hardly been the first woman to say so and probably wouldn't be the last. Time and time again, she thought about checking in with how Kelly was feeling about things, but her cowardice always won out. They had a good thing going, and she didn't want to unsettle the balance they'd managed to find. The thought of Kelly being just one more in a long string of sort-of-exes she didn't talk to anymore was too painful to contemplate. However their present arrangement came to an end, she hoped it would be amicable.

She could tell she was already in too deep when the night

finally came that Kelly left work before she did. Kelly stopped by her office to say good night. She was a sight for sore eyes since she'd stayed at her own apartment the night before, and Jillian had been in client meetings over both lunch and dinner that day. Her heart leapt when she saw Kelly in the doorway, and it was all she could do to rein in her grin to a normal level of enthusiasm.

"I'm heading out. I guess I'll go home again? Since you're still here," Kelly said.

"Okay," Jillian said. "Or…you could go to my place. I'll be at least another hour here, and Bob could use the company. You know how jumpy he gets. I think he likes having someone around."

"Are you sure?" Kelly asked uncertainly.

She wasn't at all sure, but Jillian nodded anyway. "There's an extra key somewhere in Ezra's desk."

They found it easily, and Kelly accepted it with a soft smile that was almost reverent. "I promise not to lose it. I'll see you later," she said.

Jillian lingered even longer than she strictly needed to, but finally, she was so tired that she couldn't delay going home any more. When she walked into her apartment, she was greeted by the sight of Kelly fast asleep on the couch. She'd obviously been waiting up but had dropped off. She was in sweats and an old Harvard Law T-shirt, and Bob was curled up in the crook of her arm. It was quite possibly the most wholesome thing Jillian had ever seen, and part of her wanted to live in the moment forever. The atavistic part of her brain, though, felt that old self-destructive urge to torpedo everything before it could all blow up in her face.

Kelly stirred and opened her eyes. "You're home," she said sleepily as Bob hopped down and trotted over to say hello.

It reminded Jillian of Tessa, back when she'd still bothered to wait up for her. She wanted to run out screaming into the night that this wasn't what she'd signed up for, but instead, she just helped Kelly to her feet and into the bedroom. Kelly fell back asleep almost immediately, but Jillian lay awake for a long time.

CHAPTER SEVENTEEN

The instant Kelly had asked Jillian for some closet space, she'd regretted it. She'd really only meant it from a practical standpoint—well, mostly—but she'd seen the panic in Jillian's eyes before the mask was drawn. Jillian's withdrawal for the rest of the week was the unpleasant nail in the coffin of that idea. She knew it was only logistics that prompted Jillian to change her mind, but she'd take it.

Jillian didn't ask for her key back, so Kelly held on to it. She wondered if Jillian had forgotten she had it, but she certainly wasn't about to remind her. Every time she saw it on her key ring or let herself into Jillian's apartment with it, it let her pretend that what they had was more than it was. She knew she was making things worse for herself in the long run, that it would hurt all the more whenever Jillian eventually got tired of her, but it felt too good to stop.

Although Jillian got the hang of taking care of Bob quickly, she didn't seem to mind Kelly using him as an excuse to come over more often. The little kitten had taken to both of them and seemed happiest when sitting between them being doted on. The only thing Kelly found more adorable than Bob himself was the way Jillian cooed at him lovingly, sounding utterly besotted. For someone who had declared herself not a pet person, Jillian had certainly come around.

If only she'd come around on not being a relationship person, too, Kelly thought ruefully.

She enjoyed her weekend at her mom's, and Allison's party on her actual birthday was fun. All their college friends in the area, including Dan, showed up. She felt a slight pang upon seeing him, not of regret, but more of wistfulness for a time in her life when love had seemed a lot simpler. By the time she finished her third glass of a spiked punch whose ingredients Allison refused to name, she found herself feeling distinctly maudlin. She was just drunk enough that instead of going home after the party, it seemed like a good idea to take an Uber to Jillian's instead.

Jillian had been in court and then client meetings for most of the day, so Kelly had barely seen her other than in passing. If ever she deserved to show up tipsy and unannounced to impose her presence, it was on her birthday. As she fumbled with the lock, she had the horrifying vision of finding Jillian with someone else. That would officially make this her worst birthday ever, even more than when Sarah's mom had crashed her ninth birthday party.

When she got inside, though, she found only a very surprised Jillian on the couch. She'd been flipping through legal files and petting Bob, but as soon as he saw Kelly, he leapt down to greet her, meowing in delight.

"What are you doing here?" Jillian asked, sounding confused.

"It's my birthday," Kelly told her, scooping Bob up and carrying him back to the couch.

"I know. Happy birthday," Jillian said, looking like she was trying hard not to laugh. "It sounds like you had fun at your party."

"I'm drunk," Kelly announced.

Jillian gave up fighting it and laughed openly. "Yeah, I can tell. Come sit down."

Kelly flopped next to her and rested her head on her shoulder as Bob settled half on her lap and half on Jillian's, purring like an engine. "I missed you today."

Jillian kissed the top of her head, then threaded her fingers through Kelly's hair and scritched her scalp. "I missed you, too."

"Mmm, that feels good," Kelly mumbled, leaning into her touch. "Keep doing that."

Jillian obeyed and asked, "How was your party?"

Kelly shrugged. "It was fine. Missed you."

"I know. I'm sorry I barely saw you on your birthday," Jillian said.

"Not just today," Kelly said, shaking her head vigorously. "I miss you all the time. Whenever you're not there, I always miss you."

Jillian went stock-still beside her, and Kelly thought vaguely that she'd probably regret the words once she sobered up. "You're very sweet. I'm pretty sure you're the only one who's ever thought that about me. Well, maybe Bob, too," Jillian said.

Kelly leaned up and kissed the underside of Jillian's chin. "I really love—Bob," she said, pivoting at the last second. She wasn't quite drunk enough to make *that* big a mistake.

"Me too," Jillian said after a pause. "I really do, more than I should. Come on, let's get you to bed."

❖

Kelly cursed Allison's name when she woke up the next morning, her skull feeling like it had been split in two.

Her memories of the previous night were hazy, and it took her a minute to realize where she was. She could hear Jillian singing in the shower and groaned as she looked at the clock and realized she needed to be at work in less than an hour. Jillian had set a glass of water and a bottle of Tylenol on the nightstand for her. She grasped at them blindly, wincing when she had to open her eyes to open the child safety lock.

"Good morning," Jillian said, emerging from the bathroom in a robe with her hair wrapped in a towel.

Kelly groaned again. "There's nothing good about it."

Jillian smirked. "A little too much fun last night for a weeknight, huh?"

"Way too much. How did I end up here?" Kelly asked, rubbing her forehead and willing the Tylenol to kick in.

"You don't remember anything about last night?" Jillian asked carefully as she started getting dressed.

Kelly tried to think, but it hurt her head too much. "Not really. Oh no, did I totally embarrass myself?"

"You did not," Jillian said. "We basically went straight to bed. I'm not surprised you don't remember it. Your breath smelled like a liquor store after an earthquake."

Kelly started to laugh but stopped quickly as it set her head pounding. "That's a very evocative image. I think that punch must have had some of every kind of alcohol in the world."

"Come on, up and at 'em. Only two more days and then you can fully recuperate at the lake," Jillian said briskly, helping her sit up.

Kelly brightened at the thought of a whole weekend with Jillian all to herself, not that she could say that out loud.

Somehow, she made it through work on Thursday without either falling asleep or throwing up, which she considered a minor miracle. Friday dragged on slowly, her excitement about the lake making the work day feel even longer. She and Jillian went back to their old habit of staggering their departure times, not wanting Leon to know they had weekend plans together. She wouldn't put it past him to come up with a reason for her to have to work on Saturday if he knew.

They dropped Bob off at Sarah's to spend the weekend with his sisters, then hit the road. Jillian was right, and the cabin was absolutely freezing when they got there, but she quickly got a fire going. They sat in front of it for a while until they were warm, then Jillian removed Kelly's clothes and went down on her with such tenderness, it made her heart hurt. Kelly held her afterward and let herself imagine it meant anything close to as much to Jillian as it did to her.

Although it wasn't fully frozen over yet, patches of ice had started dotting the surface of the water, and Jillian didn't think it was a good idea to go out in the canoe the next morning. Instead, they climbed one of the little mountains nearby and got a sweeping view of the lake. Jillian pointed out the island that had the little outdoor chapel that looked indistinguishable from all the others at this distance.

In the afternoon, they sat side by side in front of the fire, working on their laptops while squirrels scampered around on the roof gathering fallen acorns. Instead of going back to one of the terrible restaurants, they stayed in and had a simple dinner of canned soup and crackers.

"I'm sorry this isn't a fancier birthday dinner," Jillian said. "Although it probably tastes just as good as anything we could get in town."

Kelly laughed at that. "It's fine. I'm happy just to be here with you."

"Well, I'll take you out for a real dinner when we get back," Jillian said.

"You don't have to do that," Kelly said, surprised.

"I know I don't. I'm doing it because I want to," Jillian said grinning at her.

Kelly smiled back shyly. "Well, thank you, then," she said.

After dinner, Jillian said, "Put your coat on. I want to show you something."

Jillian grabbed the down comforter from the bed and led them down to the dock with a flashlight. It was frigid, but they wrapped themselves in the comforter and lay on their backs. Once they were settled in, Jillian clicked the flashlight off.

"Wow," Kelly said softly, staring at the night sky. She'd never seen so many stars in her life.

"It's amazing how much you can see without all the light pollution of the city," Jillian said, and Kelly could hear the smile in her voice.

"It's so beautiful," Kelly said, awestruck.

Jillian kissed her cheek. "I was hoping we'd have a clear night so you could see this."

Kelly held her close, feeling the warmth of Jillian's breath on her skin. "Thank you. It's magical," she whispered.

They lay on the dock snuggled together in the blanket under the stars for as long as they could stand the cold. Kelly could have stayed out there forever in the dark, intertwined with Jillian. It felt like they were the only people in the world or more accurately, like she was the only person in Jillian's world. Eventually, reality had to set in, and once their faces turned numb and their teeth started chattering, they gave it up and went back inside.

Jillian's face was flushed from the cold, and she looked so heartbreakingly lovely that Kelly couldn't resist pulling out her phone and taking a candid picture.

"What was that for?" Jillian asked, laughing. "I must look like a cherry Popsicle."

"You're the most beautiful thing I've ever seen," Kelly blurted without thinking, then bit her lip in embarrassment.

Jillian looked at her intently, then surged forward and pulled her into a kiss. Her lips were cold at first, but they warmed quickly as their passion built. They tugged at each other's clothes feverishly, and soon, they were both naked. Kelly felt raw desire surging through her veins, as powerful as their first night together. She pulled Jillian onto her lap, clutching at her ass while she kissed her way down her neck and took her breast into her mouth. Jillian moaned and buried her hands in Kelly's hair, grinding their hips together. Kelly slid her hand between their bodies, and Jillian gasped as Kelly started caressing her wet folds.

"Fuck, oh fuck," Jillian panted, thrusting against Kelly's hand.

Kelly slipped two fingers inside her and rubbed her clit with her thumb. Jillian raked her nails down Kelly's back, keening. It felt like no time at all before Jillian's body was gripping at Kelly's fingers as she came. When she was done, she rested her forehead on Kelly's shoulder and let out a long sigh of satisfaction before drawing her into another kiss.

Kelly returned it avidly, feeling more turned on than ever. Jillian gently pushed her onto her back and cupped her cheek, smiling down at her. Kelly's breath caught, pinned by the fondness in her gaze. It was almost enough to make her believe she was special, that Jillian really cared for her the way she wished she did.

Not really knowing what she planned to say, she opened her mouth and said, "Jillian, I—" but Jillian cut her off with a kiss, and all coherent thought fled her mind.

She moaned as Jillian moved her lips to her neck and rubbed at her nipples, then moved her hand between Kelly's legs. Kelly's hips bucked, and she cried out, pleasure rushing through her as Jillian stroked her. Jillian moved down and started lavishing her clit with her tongue as she continued sliding her fingers in and out of her. Kelly cried out wordlessly, unable to tear her eyes away from the sight.

Jillian was so familiar with her body by now that she knew exactly how to bring her right to the edge. She was so close that all it took was Jillian's eyes flicking up to meet hers before she was shrieking through a toe-curling orgasm.

She pulled Jillian up beside her and kissed her, still trying to catch her breath. Jillian held her close and petted her hair, occasionally planting soft kisses along her temple until she fell asleep.

❖

After breakfast on Sunday, Jillian went up to a small attic crawl space and brought down several boxes of photos and other memorabilia. "I don't even know what half of this is. It must be Jerome's stuff," she said. "I always meant to go through it after he died, but I never seemed to have the time."

They found Jillian's senior yearbook in one box. Kelly barely recognized her in her photo. She looked slightly underbaked, pale and almost mousy. It was hard to reconcile with the Jillian she knew today. Jillian turned up two pictures of herself proudly holding fish she'd caught, one as a child with her father and the other with Jerome when she was a teenager. In most photos, Jerome looked grumpy and taciturn, much as Jillian had described him. In the picture with her, though, he was looking at her fondly, his lips almost turned up in a smile.

Kelly reached into one of the boxes to see what else was

in there and came up with a thick packet of old letters tied together with twine. "Do you know what these are?" she asked Jillian, holding them up.

"No. They look pretty old. Go ahead and open them if you want," Jillian said, then went back to flipping through her yearbook.

Kelly shuffled through the envelopes. They were all postmarked from Ottumwa, Iowa, from someone with the initials W.L.P. She started lifting the flap of the oldest one, but her phone went off with the Wicked Witch of the West music from *The Wizard of Oz*, and she fumbled to answer it.

"Hi, Leon," she said, while Jillian tried valiantly to smother her laugh at the ringtone. Her heart sank as she listened. There had been an urgent development in one of their current cases, and he needed her in the office ASAP. She told him it would be a couple of hours, but she was on her way. By the time she hung up, Jillian was already packing.

"I'm sorry," Kelly said sadly, watching her. She bitterly regretted being pulled away from their weekend early, even for a legitimate reason.

"It's okay," Jillian said, smiling at her. "If anyone can understand, it's me. We can always come back. Let me just make sure the fire's fully out, and we can be on the road in five minutes."

"Do you want to bring any of this back with you?" Kelly asked, starting to return things to their boxes.

Jillian shrugged. "You know, that idea never occurred to me, but maybe I'll have more luck at actually getting to them if we do that. Why not? Maybe just one box for now."

Kelly placed the letters she'd been looking at back in their box and loaded it into the car along with their luggage. She looked back at the cabin as they drove away, watching until it was out of sight. Jillian had said they could come back another time, but realistically, she had to wonder if she would ever see it again.

CHAPTER EIGHTEEN

Jillian's mind raced as she drove them back to the city. She felt a mix of disappointment and relief at their getaway being cut short. The last few days had driven home the unfortunate realization that she'd fallen for Kelly. Inch by inch, Kelly had wormed her way into Jillian's heart and set up residence there. She'd felt it happening but been powerless to stop it. Well, not so much powerless as unwilling. It had all felt right in the moment, even when she knew it was a mistake that could only end in heartbreak.

After this weekend, she was pretty sure it was mutual, which made it even worse. Jillian could have continued on, quietly pining and wishing things were different if she knew Kelly was ready to pick up and move on whenever she was ready to meet someone else, someone remotely worthy of her. Kelly was so vibrant and optimistic and caring; she deserved far better than to be saddled with a jaded, neurotic, middle-aged weirdo still reeling from a busted marriage. Kelly could have met that person, who looked a lot like Dan in Jillian's mind, and gone on to be happy while Jillian licked her wounds in private.

Instead, this would go one of two ways: a clean break now or another long, torturous process like the decay of her relationship with Tessa. She couldn't do that again. She *wouldn't*. She dropped Kelly off at the office and kissed her good-bye, privately knowing this would probably be the last time she did either of those things. When Kelly came over tonight, Jillian would be a mature, reasonable adult and end things once and for all.

She felt an extra level of guilt when she picked up Bob from Sarah and Ted. She'd started to really like them, and once she broke Kelly's heart, she'd probably no longer be welcome in their lives, either. Not to mention poor little Bob, who adored Kelly possibly even more than he did Jillian. Once they got home, she threw catnip mice for him to catch and bring back to her over and over again like a dog.

"I never wanted you to grow up in a broken home," she told him, then realized how utterly ridiculous she sounded. She needed to get a grip.

To keep herself busy until Kelly got there, she started sorting through the box she'd brought back from the cabin. The letters Kelly had found were on top. For want of anything better to do, she opened one. The paper felt soft, almost fabric-like, from frequent handling. As she started reading it, her eyes went wide, and she grabbed others, flipping through them almost frantically. Sentences jumped out at her as she skimmed, using her honed speed-reading skills.

June 12, 1946
My darling Jer,

 I never thought I would long for the days of war, but that was before I had held you in my arms. Now it is 1,278 miles from my door to yours, I feel every one of them...
 Love always,
 B.

October 7, 1949
Jer darling,

Our time together was short, but you loom large in my memory. I had cognac last night, and the taste of one drop brought me right back to Normandy and Alsace...Every day I think of those nights together, those stolen moments, and dream of what might have been...

Your loving
B.

July 19, 1966
Dearest Jer,

Your last letter brought a smile to my face...I fear I've become bitter and angry, unable to think of anything but how unfair it is that we cannot be together or see each other because of the risk. Even writing as openly as we do could be dangerous, I know, but I cannot bear the thought of not being open with you, my heart, my only love...

Love always,
B.

December 1, 1992
My dear Jer,

You asked me to include a recent photo. I hate for you to see me like this, all wizened and decrepit. The truth is, I'd much rather you remember me as I was, dashing and handsome as all get-out. But you always knew I could never deny you anything.

I'm sorry to hear of all the trouble you are facing from the town. Your young friend Jillian sounds like a lone beacon of light. Your photo with her filled me with mingled joy and sadness. She could be our granddaughter if only the world were different.

We have certainly come a long way. My nephew knows two fellows living openly together in Des Moines. Right here in Iowa. Imagine that. It may be too late for us but not for Jillian. You've written so much of her, I feel like I know her already. I hope you are able to help her love who she loves without fear.

Love always,

B.

Jillian sank back against the back of the couch, feeling like a marionette whose strings had been cut. She knew who the sender must have been: William Price, Bill to his friends, Jerome's closest buddy from the Army. Apparently, he had been a lot more. There were dozens of letters in the pile, and she thought she remembered seeing more back at the cabin.

She'd had no idea, absolutely none. Sure, she'd noticed a particular fondness when he talked about Bill, but never had she imagined the depth of their relationship. Of course, Jerome rarely told her anything personal, but she'd always chalked that up to a combination of wartime PTSD and classic New Englander repression.

Conversely, Jerome had read her like a book, even before she knew the truth about herself. Tears pricked her eyes as she reread the one mentioning her. Clearly, Jerome had written about her before. The thought of him caring enough about her to tell Bill all about her set the tears flowing openly down her cheeks. She had to grab a tissue to keep from staining the paper. Bob looked up at her in concern and rammed his little head into her hand. She laughed a little through her tears and petted him. Kelly had told her animals were good at picking up human emotions, often recognizing when their owners needed comfort.

Kelly. Kelly, whom she loved. Kelly, whose heart she was planning to break tonight. Jerome and Bill couldn't have been together because society wasn't prepared to accept them. Not that they were living in a utopia now, but compared to what Jerome and Bill would have faced in the forties...

The only thing holding her back from being with Kelly was fear, fear that she might hurt her. Her eyes zeroed in on the last line of Bill's letter. *Help her love who she loves without fear.*

She held Bob close and rubbed her cheek against his soft fur, her heart racing. The truth was that she *was* afraid. She was fucking terrified. What if she took the chance and messed it up? What if she ruined Kelly's life? Her entire professional career was built on being able to see a situation from all angles, on rooting out every possible outcome. She could spend an eternity thinking of what-ifs while her actual life passed her by.

She paced back and forth, Bill's letter clutched in her hand. One minute, she felt ready to commit, the next, to run away as fast as she could. When she heard Kelly's key in the lock, her already accelerated heart rate kicked into overdrive.

"Hey! Oh man, you won't believe what happ—are you okay?" Kelly looked at her with concern. "You look like you've seen a ghost."

"I love you," Jillian said. The sight of Kelly rendered the hours of mental debate pointless. What other choice could she possibly make with Kelly right in front of her?

Kelly had dropped to her knees to pet Bob. Her mouth fell open, and she stared up at Jillian. "I...you...what? Oh, you were talking to Bob. I'm sorry, I—"

Jillian crossed the room in a flash and pulled her upright again. "I wasn't talking to Bob, although I love him too. I was telling you, Kelly Lattimore, that I, Jillian Briggs, love you. Am *in love* with you. As unfortunate and ill-advised as that is for you."

Kelly's eyes were wide, and she seemed frozen in place. All the blood left Jillian's face as she contemplated the horrifying prospect that she'd misinterpreted Kelly's feelings and had now humiliated herself for nothing. Then Kelly yanked her into a bone-crushing hug, and the fear left her.

"Do you really mean it?" Kelly whispered in her ear, still holding her so tight, it was hard to breathe.

"I really do," Jillian confirmed. Kelly loosened her grip enough that Jillian could kiss her roughly. There was no subtlety or finesse to it, just a frantic attempt to pour in every ounce of love and yearning she was feeling.

Kelly returned it fervidly, then said, "In case that wasn't clear, I love you too," before kissing her again.

Jillian had always thought *weak at the knees* was just an expression, but she found herself sagging in Kelly's arms, too overwhelmed to stand up straight. Kelly laughed quietly and helped her to the couch, where Bob hopped up to his usual spot between them. Maybe taking the bold step of actually admitting anything about her feelings to another human being *hadn't* been a huge mistake.

"Oh, I need to show you something. Look at these," she said, handing Kelly a few of Bill's letters.

"Wow," Kelly said softly. "Did you know?"

Jillian shook her head. "No. I knew he'd never been married, I just figured...he'd never met the right woman or something."

"I know it must have been rough earlier, but by the nineties, maybe they could've been together," Kelly said musingly.

"There's no way to know for sure, but I'd imagine it was hard to shake the fear of shame and stigma they must've grown up with. Maybe they just felt like it was too late by then," Jillian speculated.

"That's really sad," Kelly said, putting her arm around Jillian and resting her head on her shoulder.

Jillian reached around and petted her cheek, savoring the feel of her soft skin. "Have I mentioned that I love you?" she asked.

Kelly beamed. "You have, but you're welcome to say it as often as you want to."

"I love you," Jillian said.

"*I* love *you*," Kelly said.

They smiled at each other, and Jillian forgot what they'd been talking about, what day it was, or anything else except how much she needed Kelly's lips on hers. They eventually migrated to the bedroom, shedding clothes along the way. When they finally came up for air, they ordered dinner.

"I know I said I'd take you out for your birthday, but will you accept a rain check?" Jillian asked.

"Of course," Kelly said with a nod. "I don't want to be out of this bed any longer than we need to be. I think we have time for one more round before the food gets here."

Jillian grinned and pounced on her again.

❖

It was a lot harder to keep up their professional personas at work now that they were together for real. Serena didn't bother pretending to be surprised, smugly saying she'd seen it coming since the beginning. Ezra expressed delight that whatever Jillian had planned on her own for Kelly's birthday had apparently gone over so well.

Jillian realized she'd never actually given Kelly the gift she'd bought for her, but it no longer seemed like such a good idea now that they were actually dating.

"Well, now I'm even more curious, so you *have* to give it to me," Kelly insisted when Jillian mentioned her hesitation.

Jillian sighed. Kelly had her so fully wrapped around her little finger, it was ridiculous. She couldn't deny her anything. "Okay, fine, but I'm going to get you something more romantic, too."

She got the box from her closet and handed it over, then watched nervously as Kelly opened it. Kelly's jaw fell open as she took out the package of dark blue shibari rope Jillian had bought her.

"It's kind of a self-serving gift too, obviously," Jillian said. "And I bought a subscription to this website with online classes so we can learn how to do it together because I don't really know much about it, but the website said it was good for building intimacy and trust, and I thought maybe you'd like it, but it looks like you hate it. I can take it back and get you something else."

Kelly pressed her hand gently to Jillian's mouth to cut off her babbling. "First of all, I love it. Just because we're dating now doesn't mean I'm any less interested in the more… adventurous stuff. Plus, I love that we're getting to explore something new to both of us together. What could be more romantic than that?"

Jillian beamed and kissed her. "Great, that saves me the cost of another present."

"No," Kelly said, aghast. "I was promised another one! You just said, and I quote, 'I'm going to get you something more romantic *too*.' Emphasis mine."

"This is why I don't usually date lawyers," Jillian said, rolling her eyes.

Kelly waved that off. "Oh, you know you love me," she said.

"Yeah," Jillian said, smiling again. "I really do."

❖

"I'd successfully avoided this particular stereotype for my entire life, but she's finally turned me into a U-Haul lesbian," Jillian grumbled one day in Serena's office.

"Yeah, you look really miserable about it," Serena said drily, smirking.

"Oh, it's terrible," Jillian said, unable to hide her grin behind her coffee mug.

Maybe it was because of all the time they'd already spent together, but Jillian found herself surprisingly calm about being in an actual relationship again. Kelly continued staying at Jillian's apartment most nights, and she soon began putting her own stamp on it. Instead of the borderline-hotel art that had come with the place, she hung pictures of Bob, the lake, and even the one of Ranger with the kittens that Sarah had given her. Rather than filling Jillian with dread, the sight made her smile every time she saw it.

Best of all was the feeling of Kelly's presence whether she left the office with Jillian, was working late, or, increasingly rarely, went back to her own apartment. The indentation from her head on her pillow, the cheap Trader Joe's wine in the refrigerator, even the blond hairs caught in the drain trap, made the previously barren apartment feel like a real home. The thought was so sappy, it made Jillian want to gag, but instead, she just gave in to the inevitable and cleared out a full half of the closet for Kelly.

❖

"When I promised you a grand gesture or a favor, I was picturing something more like hiring a blimp to declare my undying love for you or having someone killed," Jillian said, staring at the jumbled mess on her living room floor. "This *really* wasn't what I had in mind."

"A favor isn't a favor if you're only doing something you want to do already," Kelly chided. She flipped through the manual again. "Do you speak any Swedish? Maybe it makes more sense than the English instructions. Or maybe if I hold the picture upside down?"

"You do know I would've happily bought you a bookshelf from a real furniture store that came assembled and made from actual wood, right?" Jillian grumbled, trying once again to make sense of the scrambled pile of screws, washers, and who knew what else.

Kelly eyed her sternly. "Don't be a snob. IKEA *is* a real furniture store. Besides, you should be happy I want to buy things for myself. Now you know I'm not just into you for your money."

"No, you're interested in my other assets," Jillian said with a smirk, twirling her ponytail and batting her eyelashes playfully.

Kelly rolled her eyes, but Jillian caught her bashful grin before she forced her expression back into seriousness. "Stop messing around. The sooner we get this done, the sooner I can put my books away and we can do something fun instead."

"Yes, ma'am," Jillian said, saluting her before going back to trying to make a one-fourth inch screw fit into a one-eighth inch hole.

With a lot of swearing, some sweat, and fending off Bob's tireless efforts to "help," they finally got the bookshelf assembled.

"I know it's not as nice as something you would've bought, but I'm proud of it," Kelly said, admiring their handiwork.

"It's not bad at all," Jillian said, watching fondly as Kelly set her well-worn *Chronicles of Narnia* box set on the top shelf. As she stood up, a flash of light caught her eye. She reached down and scooped up a single screw that they'd missed, then held it out to Kelly. They stared at it, then at each other. "You're the IKEA expert. Do we need to worry about this?" Jillian asked.

"They put in extras all the time. I'm sure it's fine," Kelly said. "It seems sturdy enough."

That task finished, they indulged themselves in a variety of much more fun activities for the rest of the evening. Kelly dozed off after, Bob nestled contentedly against her in a little spoon position and snoring away.

Jillian was well on her way to joining them in slumber when a loud crash filled the air. She sat bolt upright in bed, her heart racing.

"Wuzzat?" Kelly said groggily, looking around.

Jillian grabbed the baseball bat she kept behind her nightstand just in case. "Dial nine, one, and have your finger over the one key," she hissed, handing Kelly her phone.

"Jillian, don't. It could be dangerous," she whispered urgently.

Jillian waved her off and crept toward the bedroom door, bat at the ready. She took a deep breath, then flung it open and charged into the living room.

Enough moonlight was coming in through the uncovered windows that she could make out dark rectangles all over the floor. She couldn't see anyone moving, so she cautiously flipped on the light. As soon as the sight before her registered in her brain, she started laughing.

"Is everything okay?" Kelly asked, tiptoeing out of the bedroom behind her. "Oh no." She bent to retrieve her copy of *The Horse and His Boy*, which had been flung nearly across the room from the force with which the bookshelf had collapsed.

Jillian laughed even harder at the look of dismay on Kelly's face.

"It's not funny," Kelly snapped. "That was terrifying. And my books…"

"They're…fine," Jillian gasped in between chuckles.

"I guess so," Kelly said, gathering them up and examining them one by one. "I never would have thought one missing screw could cause so much damage. Will you stop laughing already?" She attempted to scowl, but a giggle escaped, and they both collapsed on the couch in laughter, looking at the wreckage of their earlier handiwork.

After the adrenaline rush of the sudden noise died off, they piled Kelly's books up in neat stacks on the floor and went back to bed. Bob, who normally jumped up to investigate the slightest sound, merely blinked at them disinterestedly and went back to sleep.

"It's a good thing that wasn't really an intruder. Some guard cat you turned out to be. You're of no use whatsoever," Jillian told him in disgust.

"Seriously," Kelly said. "The last time I used the microwave, he freaked out at the beep, but he had zero reaction to that? At least he's decorative."

Jillian pulled Kelly close, breathing in her scent. "I guess I'm not that useful, either, since I can't put together a bookshelf without causing chaos."

"You have other purposes, though," Kelly said, leaning into her touch.

"Like buying you a real bookshelf?" Jillian teased.

"Mmm-hmm," Kelly said sleepily. "Besides, you're decorative too. Extremely decorative."

"Truly the best compliment I've ever received," Jillian said.

"I don't know, I still think the best thing about you is your taste in women," Kelly said with a snicker.

Jillian laughed. "Eleanor's" response to her flirty first message felt like a lifetime ago. "It's good to know you aren't suffering from low self-esteem. If you were, I'd have to make sure to tell you how smart"—she planted a kiss on Kelly's temple—"and funny"—she kissed Kelly's cheek—"and sexy"—she kissed Kelly's neck—"and kind and good and amazing you are." She finished by kissing Kelly's shoulder, then wrapped her arms around her and squeezed her tight. "So actually, I think you might be right about me having good taste."

"I'm always right," Kelly said smugly.

"Not about putting together stuff from IKEA," Jillian fired back.

"Oh, that was low. You'll pay for that one, Briggs," Kelly said, furrowing her eyebrows in an adorable attempt to seem menacing.

"I'll be quaking in my boots," Jillian said, somehow managing to keep a straight face. "Guess I'll have to make it up to you somehow."

"Tell me you love me," Kelly said.

"I love you," Jillian said.

Kelly kissed her cheek. "Okay, we're square now."

"That was easy."

"Not as easy as you are."

"You take that back, Kelly Lattimore!"

"Make me."

"Don't let your mouth write checks your ass can't cash," Jillian warned.

"I think you've seen by now that that's not a problem," Kelly said, giggling. "I can't help it if I'm perfect."

Jillian laughed too, squeezing Kelly as tightly as she could. "You may not be perfect, but you're perfect for me."

EPILOGUE

A re we ready? They'll be here any minute," Kelly called, checking her makeup in the hallway mirror.

"We're set. All that's missing is our guests—Bob, get down! I'm going to put you in jail if you keep doing that," Jillian yelled from the dining room.

Kelly grinned, knowing Bob must have once again climbed onto the table. "Jail" was the guest room, complete with litter box, food, toys, and a number of soft cat beds, but he considered it cruel beyond belief.

There was a knock at the door, and she opened it to admit her sister and newly minted brother-in-law. Hellos and hugs were exchanged all around, including with their newest foster dog, Popcorn. Sarah finally seemed ready to open her heart to a new dog, and Kelly and Jillian were hoping Popcorn would be a foster fail. Not only was she a sweetheart, but she and Bob loved playing together.

"Congratulations again," Jillian said to Ted and Sarah. "Come sit down and tell us all about the honeymoon."

The joy was evident in Sarah and Ted's faces as they talked about their trip to Bali. "We got the proofs of the wedding pictures back, too," Sarah said. "Do you want to see them? I'm still sorry you couldn't be there."

"It's fine," Kelly assured her.

Sarah's mom still wanted nothing to do with Kelly, so Sarah and Kelly had mutually agreed that she and Jillian would sit the wedding out and celebrate with them afterward. Kelly truly didn't mind; she knew Sarah was walking a difficult line, and some battles just weren't worth fighting. Even their dad wasn't terribly happy about their reunion, finding it awkward and strange. Jillian had some choice words for Benton about that, which was why Kelly kept the two of them apart as much as possible.

"You guys leave on Sunday, right? What time are you dropping Bob off?" Sarah asked after dinner.

"Around eight a.m., if that works for you," Jillian said, and Sarah nodded.

"It's not exactly Bali, but I'm really excited for this trip," Kelly said.

"I'm surprised you could get the time off, Jillian. How's life at the firm?" Ted asked.

"It's been great," Jillian said. "One of Leon's biggest clients asked to work with me exclusively. It utterly crushed his morale. I almost feel bad for him."

Kelly rolled her eyes. "Oh please, you've been gloating about it all week."

"You've got me there," Jillian admitted, and all four of them laughed. "I do miss seeing Kelly at work, though."

She smiled at Kelly, and Kelly felt familiar butterflies as she smiled back. She didn't think she'd ever get tired of Jillian looking at her with such love and fondness in her eyes.

It was true that they saw each other less during the day now that Kelly was working at a nonprofit that represented seniors in elder abuse cases. After a year at the firm, Jillian had sat Kelly down and insisted she look for another job, one that didn't make her miserable.

"But my loans," Kelly protested.

"We'll figure it out," Jillian said firmly.

"I can't ask that of you," Kelly insisted.

Jillian looked at her sternly. "You didn't ask, I'm offering to help. Besides, I have a plan."

A few days later, Jillian mysteriously disappeared for several hours. By the time they were sitting on the couch after dinner, Kelly got a notification that her loan balance was now zero.

"What did you do?" she asked Jillian, slightly afraid of what the answer would be.

Jillian had the good grace to look mildly guilty. "I may have happened upon Benton at a hotel with a woman who was definitely not Mrs. Lattimore and, let's say, suggested that it might behoove him to pay off your loans."

"So basically, you blackmailed him," Kelly said, trying to sound disapproving and failing utterly. "What, were you having him followed or something?"

"The firm has a number of investigators on staff who assist with a variety of cases," Jillian said primly. "I simply called in a favor."

"Wow, that was an expensive hotel visit for him. And pointless, too. From what Sarah says, her mom already knows. She just doesn't care enough anymore to do anything about it," Kelly said.

Jillian sighed. "That's a little sad, isn't it? To just bury your head in the sand and accept it? Although I guess that's kind of what I did with Tessa, so I'm not one to talk."

Kelly held her close while Bob tried to wedge himself into the nonexistent space between them. Somehow, he managed it, defying both physics and social norms about personal space.

"I love you," she told Jillian.

"Were you talking to Bob?" Jillian asked, gently teasing her.

"You know perfectly well I was talking to you," Kelly said, kissing her.

❖

The day of their trip finally arrived. Jillian looked calm on the surface, but Kelly could tell she was tense as their plane pulled up to the gate of the Des Moines airport. Kelly managed to distract her for most of the drive, but by the time they reached the exit for Ottumwa, she was as anxious as Jillian. They found the address they were looking for and walked up to the front door of the neatly kept brick ranch house. The door was opened on the first knock by a gray-haired man in a sweater-vest with a friendly smile.

"Hi, I'm Carl Price. Welcome!" He ushered them inside.

They introduced themselves, and he led them to a cozy living room. He offered them coffee, but they declined. Kelly didn't know about Jillian, but she herself was on edge enough without caffeine.

"I brought out everything I could find," Carl said. "We lost a few boxes when our basement flooded a few years back, but I think most of Uncle Bill's stuff escaped unscathed. And of course, he himself did, too." He pointed to an urn on the mantel.

They spent the afternoon with Carl in his dining room, matching Bill and Jerome's letters up by date. They hadn't been able to bring all the physical copies of Bill's letters, but they'd scanned the rest of them onto Kelly's laptop. Bill and Jerome had written each other faithfully every week from the end of the war until Bill died in 1998. At various points, both

Jillian and Carl wept, and Kelly found herself tearing up too, even after having never met the two men. Carl ran his hands over one of the letters they'd brought.

"It's good to see his handwriting again," he explained. "I have a few things, grocery lists and things like that, but nothing like this. He raised me after my parents died, did you know that?"

Kelly and Jillian shook their heads. That was probably another reason why Bill wouldn't have wanted to come out or live openly with Jerome. They insisted on leaving some of Bill's letters with Carl and took a few of Jerome's in exchange.

Jillian was quiet in the hotel that night.

"How are you feeling?" Kelly asked.

Jillian shrugged, then flopped beside Kelly on the bed and burrowed into her shoulder. "Kind of...guilty? We're living this great life, and they couldn't, through no fault of their own."

"I know what you mean," Kelly said. "But I think they'd just want us to be happy. Hey, I have an idea."

She explained it, and Jillian beamed.

❖

A few days after they flew back, they drove up to the lake. They paddled out to the island chapel in an almost reverent silence. They walked hand in hand down the path and up the aisle.

"The next time we do this, we'll be wearing much less comfortable shoes," Jillian said. The chapel caretaker was an old friend of Jerome's and had pulled some strings to get them a wedding date without sitting through the usual two-year waiting list.

Kelly squeezed her hand, and they moved to the altar. A light breeze was blowing as they stepped out onto a huge rock that went out right over the water.

"You ready?" Kelly asked.

Jillian sighed heavily. "No, but I won't ever be. No time like the present."

She opened the box that contained half of Jerome's ashes and half of Bill's, mingled together. The other halves were back in Iowa on Carl's mantel. Carl had loved Kelly's suggestion of mixing the ashes as much as Jillian had. Kelly took her hand and squeezed it reassuringly. Jillian smiled nervously.

"You, uh, know dumping ashes like this is illegal, right?" Kelly said, not wanting to mar the solemnity of the moment.

Jillian smiled. "Jerome's philosophy was, it's only illegal if someone catches you. In a way, this is a good way to honor him."

"Do you want to say a few words?" Kelly asked.

"It's more in the spirit of Jerome to grunt and nod," Jillian said. "Besides, I wouldn't know what to say."

"Let's just say good-bye, then," Kelly said. "Jerome and Bill, I hope you're together again and happy, wherever you are."

The tenderness and affection in Jillian's eyes almost knocked Kelly off her feet. "Well said," Jillian said, slightly mistily. She gently poured the box of ashes out into the lake, the breeze picking them up and scattering them.

Back in the cabin that night, they made love voraciously. When they were finally spent, they lay awake for a long time, their sweat-slick limbs intertwined.

"Oh God," Jillian said, sounding horrified.

"What is it?" Kelly asked sleepily.

"I just realized...we essentially have *Leon* to thank for our relationship," Jillian said with a shudder. "I really doubt we would have gotten together if we hadn't spent your first two weeks working together. All thanks to Leon and his stupid ankle."

Kelly giggled, both at the thought and at the look of revulsion on Jillian's face. "We should write him a thank-you note. Maybe send a gift basket."

"I'm not sure I'm physically capable of keeping myself from poisoning the contents of a gift basket," Jillian mused.

"I bet you could if you tried," Kelly teased.

Jillian leaned over and kissed her on the tip of her nose. "Yeah, I probably could. After all, I have a lot to be grateful for."

About the Author

Cassidy Crane has always enjoyed coming up with stories but only recently started writing them down. By day she is a librarian, by night an avid reader, crafter, sports fan, and cat servant. She lives in New England with her wife and their two feline overlords.

Books Available From Bold Strokes Books

The First Kiss by Patricia Evans. As the intrigue surrounding her latest case spins dangerously out of control, military police detective Parker Haven must choose between her career and the woman she's falling in love with. (978-1-63679-775-5)

Language Lessons by Sage Donnell. Grace and Lenka never expected to fall in love. Is home really where the heart is if it means giving up your dreams? (978-1-63679-725-0)

New Horizons by Shia Woods. When Quinn Collins meets Alex Anders, Horizon Theater's enigmatic managing director, a passionate connection ignites, but amidst the complex backdrop of theater politics, their budding romance faces a formidable challenge. (978-1-63679-683-3)

Scrambled: A Tuesday Night Book Club Mystery by Jaime Maddox. Avery Hutchins makes a discovery about her father's death that will force her to face an impossible choice between doing what is right and finally finding a way to regain a part of herself she had lost. (978-1-63679-703-8)

Stolen Hearts by Michele Castleman. Finding the thief who stole a precious heirloom will become Ella's first move in a dangerous game of wits that exposes family secrets and could lead to her family's financial ruin. (978-1-63679-733-5)

Synchronicity by J.J. Hale. Dance, destiny, and undeniable passion collide at a summer camp as Haley and Cal navigate a love story that intertwines past scars with present desires. (978-1-63679-677-2)

Wild Fire by Radclyffe & Julie Cannon. When Olivia returns to the Red Sky Ranch, Riley's carefully crafted safe world goes up in flames. Can they take a risk and cross the fire line to find love? (978-1-63679-727-4)

Writ of Love by Cassidy Crane. Kelly and Jillian struggle to navigate the ruthless battleground of Big Law, grappling with desire, ambition, and the thin line between success and surrender. (978-1-63679-738-0)

Back to Belfast by Emma L. McGeown. Two colleagues are asked to trade jobs. Claire moves to Vancouver and Stacie moves to Belfast, and though they've never met in person, they can't seem to escape a growing attraction from afar. (978-1-63679-731-1)

The Breakdown by Ronica Black. Vaughn and Natalie have chemistry, but the outside world keeps knocking at the door, threatening more trouble, making the love and the life they want together impossible. (978-1-63679-675-8)

The Curse by Alexandra Riley. Can Diana Dillon and her daughter, Ryder, survive the cursed farm with the help of Deputy Mel Defoe? Or will the land choose them to be the next victims? (978-1-63679-611-6)

Exposure by Nicole Disney & Kimberly Cooper Griffin. For photographer Jax Bailey and delivery driver Trace Logan, keeping it casual is a matter of perspective. (978-1-63679-697-0)

Hunt of Her Own by Elena Abbott. Finding forever won't be easy, but together Danaan's and Ashly's paths lead back to the supernatural sanctuary of Terabend. (978-1-63679-685-7)

Perfect by Kris Bryant. They say opposites attract, but Alix and Marianna have totally different dreams. No Hollywood love story is perfect, right? (978-1-63679-601-7)

Royal Expectations by Jenny Frame. When childhood sweethearts Princess Teddy Buckingham and Summer Fisher reunite, their feelings resurface and so does the public scrutiny that tore them apart. (978-1-63679-591-1)

Shadow Rider by Gina L. Dartt. In the Shadows, one can easily find death, but can Shay and Keagan find love as they fight to save the Five Nations? (978-1-63679-691-8)

Tribute by L.M. Rose. To save her people, Fiona will be the tribute in a treaty marriage to the Tipruii princess, Simaala, and spend the rest of her days on the other side of the wall between their races. (978-1-63679-693-2)

Wild Wales by Patricia Evans. When Finn and Aisling fall in love, they must decide whether to return to the safety of the lives they had, or take a chance on wild love in windswept Wales. (978-1-63679-771-7)